Habitat Creation

in GARDEN DESIGN

A guide
to designing places for people and wildlife

Catherine Heatherington & Alex Johnson

Habitat Creation
in GARDEN DESIGN

A guide
to designing places for people and wildlife

THE CROWOOD PRESS

First published in 2022 by
The Crowood Press Ltd
Ramsbury, Marlborough
Wiltshire SN8 2HR

enquiries@crowood.com

www.crowood.com

British Library Cataloguing-in-Publication Data
A catalogue record for this book is available from the British Library.

ISBN 978 0 7198 4096 8

Dedication
For fellow wildlife watchers and designers of the future.

Typeset by Chennai Publishing Services
Cover design by Sergey Tsvetkov
Printed and bound in India by Parksons Graphics

CONTENTS

ACKNOWLEDGEMENTS

The seeds for this book were sown when we were selected to design a wildlife garden for the RSPB in 2009. We have abiding affection for that garden, and gratitude to the staff with whom we worked there, particularly Jane Warren and Shirley Boyle who continues to nurture it with enthusiastic volunteers.

We have had advice that we haven't always taken, encouragement that we often needed and enthusiasm from unexpected sources. We have been grateful for it all, even when it didn't appear so.

Many people have supported us along the way, first and foremost our families – Larry Mindel and David Johnson, Ellie, Beth, Rosie and George.

All the photos were taken by Catherine Heatherington and Alex Johnson unless otherwise stated. Thank you to the photographers who generously allowed us to use their work in this book: Paul Tierney, Marianne Majerus, Sergio Denche (especially for his photo at the beginning of Chapter 1), Ellie Mindel, Beth Mindel-Holmes, Oli Holmes, Paul Dracott, Wendy Allen, William Martin, Adam Clarke and Alison Gouldstone.

We would especially like to thank Paul Dracott, Dermot Foley and James Fox who were generous enough to contribute details and photos of their designs.

We are very grateful to our many clients who have been generous in letting us make free with their gardens and maintaining them in a condition in which we still like to photograph them. Where gardens photographed are open to the public, we have identified them. For others we thank the owners and respect their privacy.

Thank you to our colleagues in design, horticulture and ecology who have answered our questions and provided material that we have used – Rosi Rollings, Wendy Allen, Sophie Coles, and to our friends who have advised us, offered suggestions and asked pertinent questions, especially Alison and Angela.

And, finally, to The Crowood Press who have been supportive with encouragement and sound advice throughout; we offer our gratitude.

PREFACE

The area of Britain covered by gardens is difficult to ascertain: the Royal Horticultural Society (RHS) (2021e) estimates it is about 270,000 hectares. Whatever the figure, it is clear that this is a huge resource. Many garden owners would like to attract wildlife, and there is plenty of advice from organizations such as the Royal Horticultural Society (RHS), the Royal Society for the Protection of Birds (RSPB), the Wildlife Trusts and the Woodland Trust on how to achieve this. There are instructions for constructing ponds and bee hotels. There are numerous lists of bee-friendly flowers. And there is a plethora of artefacts to buy to attract birds, creepy crawlies, hedgehogs and even bats.

The time is right, therefore, to consider how we can design gardens that integrate this wealth of advice with fundamental design principles to create aesthetically pleasing spaces with diverse habitats that support a range of plants and creatures.

Throughout this book we will show how habitats can be productive and valuable without having to compromise on design and aesthetics. Along the way we will examine some of the recent research in the field and seek to inspire readers to take some of our suggestions and experiment for themselves. In approaching design we always remember that a garden is a habitat for people as well as other creatures. It is important to stress that these are not wild places, although they do support wild things. However, as we will show, these wild things do not mind if we design spaces that are contemporary or even formal as long as their needs are met.

There is a tendency to equate messiness with naturalness and the idea that wildlife gardens need to be untidy and unkempt (and have a nettle patch) persists even though there is research that shows this need not be the case (Gaston *et al.*, 2005). In some respects ecosystems are messy: vegetation intermingles, brambles scramble and engulf, leaf litter and fallen branches decompose. But there are other cases where we see patterns in the dispersion of perennials and the tapestry of moorland, in the horizontality of a carpet of bluebells and the vertical forms of trees. We will discuss how to balance the desire for a garden that looks attractive throughout the year with the need for some measure of untidiness.

Landscape architect and academic, Joan Iverson Nassauer's (1995) influential paper, 'Messy ecosystems, orderly frames', was written nearly three decades ago but much of what she says remains relevant today. She points to the necessity of designing 'cues to care' that 'provide a cultural context for ecological function' (Nassauer, 1995: p.161). These cues draw attention away from the appearance of messiness, indicating that the ecosystem is, in some way, cared for. At its simplest this could be mowing an edge strip along a hedgerow or a path through a meadow, as suggested even before Nassauer by ecologist Oliver Gilbert (1989).

In this book we use the language of design to frame garden habitats. Thus they become not only more acceptable to people visiting the garden, but also more comprehensible. An understanding of the processes involved in even the smallest of habitats encourages people to value ecosystems outside the garden where they may be dismissed as merely messy and uncared for. As Nassauer says, 'Invisible ecological function must be actively represented for human experience if human beings are to maintain ecological quality' (1995: p.163).

Gardens face many threats: they may be built on; housing in new developments is usually high density, leaving less green space; and the amount of hard land-scaping, particularly in front gardens, is increasing (Thompson and Head, 2020). The loss of biodiversity around the world is massive – scientists speak of an ongoing sixth mass extinction (Ceballos *et al.*, 2017) – and the climate crisis can only make matters worse. Up to one million species are threatened with extinction, some within a matter of decades (United Nations, 2019). This is not something that we can solve in our gardens. They are not places in which to protect or reintroduce endangered species (Thompson, 2007). Nevertheless, when gardens are connected across towns or cities, they have the potential to form an extensive vegetated area and thus support a huge range of habitats.

It is important to point out that this book is solely about gardens: it is not about creating habitats in nature reserves or about returning places to nature or about rewilding. We are not trying to replicate natural places, and the suggestions we make about plant choices and other interventions are specifically made with gardens in mind.

We will show, in the following chapters, how gardens have the potential to support and benefit plants and creatures, together with their human visitors, and how they can be enjoyed while also educating and inspiring. And, most of all, we hope that by experiencing and working with legible habitat gardens we will all gain a better understanding of our interconnectedness with wild things and places.

In his garden in France, Mark Brown uses hedges, mown paths and a grid of fruit trees to frame the meadow and an exuberant mix of perennials.

CHAPTER 1

ECOLOGY

In the course of two generations the word ecology has taken on a much wider remit and is used in very broad terms. It is a field of study rather than a perfect system, and we may have to study imperfect systems. The focus of this book is design in gardens, and marrying design with good environmental practice to achieve maximum biodiversity. At its simplest, ecology can be distilled to why organisms live where they do. They do not choose to live there; they are bound to live there by their adaptation through evolution over millennia. They may be forced though adverse conditions to the margins of those places, and may either adapt further or go extinct.

Our gardens, fortunately, are unlikely to be responsible for extinctions, but we can design them to provide places where animals and plants can find conditions promising for their survival. In design we select forms, colours and growth patterns in plants that support our concepts, and we frequently need to tinker with the growing environment to ensure that they thrive. Unhealthy plants are neither attractive nor are they beneficial to wildlife. A garden has the potential to be a place that is abundant in its variety of mood, visual delight and ecological richness. In creating or sustaining habitats, the denseness of the vegetation and its persistence are central, and the variety of conditions under which different plants will thrive underpins this. Understanding the needs of plants and how they

Blackthorn growing at the edge of its habitat, showing an extreme soil profile.

Rich flush of spring flowers before the leaf canopy becomes dense, with moss on an aging pollard bole.

Harebells finding root runs between rocks; the rate of change of this habitat will be slow.

interact establishes some parameters for design, stimulates ideas and reminds us of appropriate associations of plants and materials. Far from limiting creativity, it reinforces a sense of place.

Why does an organism live where it does now and not last week, last year or last century? Change is fundamental to ecology. In observing nature we see a snapshot of what is happening now, but the situation is unlikely to be stable, even though the time frame in which we see it may make it seem so. Every community is in flux, with populations rising and falling in response to conditions, each of which has consequential effects.

Conditions for Survival

Living conditions, both in the wild and in cultural landscapes, are rarely ideal and what we observe is how organisms have adapted to thrive in certain environments, including the ways in which they overcome adverse elements within them. For plants, the intensity of light, moisture and nutrients are limiting factors, but so is competition from other plants for those necessities.

Every community includes predators – the most dominant is called the apex predator – which have a part to play in population control. In gardens these are most likely to be species of birds. Magpies and jays are common, but sparrowhawks and kestrels may make an appearance, as may grass snakes. Predation also comes in the form of tiny aggressors – the greenflies, spiders, slugs and caterpillars. The strategies that plants and animals use to counteract or compensate for predation include reproducing prolifically, remaining hidden for much of the day or sending out new shoots to replace those eaten, and more dramatic protection in the form of spines, poisons and irritants, as well as biochemical reactions (Walling, 2000).

Requirements and Habitats

The basic requirements that organisms need to survive are food, water and shelter. To have access to these they need sufficient territory in order to find them in adequate quantities. Light of the right intensity is important to many plants and animals and is key to many daily and seasonal rhythms in their lives. Gaseous oxygen for respiration is the most critical component for almost every organism; it is unlikely to be limiting in gardens, unless flooding, poor drainage or soil compaction occurs.

Habitats contain the conditions that a plant or animal needs to make its home. A habitat for a bird of prey or a wolf may stretch to many square kilometres and encompass different sorts of terrain and vegetation. Crawling insects seek habitats that have exacting requirements, but can be very small in physical space, whilst flying insects may have similar requirements, occupying habitats that are more diffuse. Organisms all occupy ecological niches. A niche describes the role it plays in the environment but also how the organism responds to the distribution of resources and its interaction with competitors and predators. Two different species that have identical niches also have identical requirements for survival and cannot stably co-exist. Habitats do not exist in isolation, they join up with other habitats and may overlap them, but eventually they have an edge. Plants may cast their seeds and pollen to drift on the wind to find a suitable habitat further afield, but small animals have to fly, jump or risk crossing inhospitable habitats. In later chapters we will discuss corridors and other ways in which designers can facilitate the movement of animals.

Polypodium cambricum growing in thin pockets of soil on a rock outcrop where there is little competition, at the University of Bristol Botanic Garden.

Competition and Evolution

The circumstances that make food, shelter and water available are complex and variable. It is the variables of these conditions and competition for them that make the habitats that favour different organisms. In the garden, competition is largely managed to favour the plants we select, and plants that would not succeed in the wild are given the water and nutrients they require, placed in the appropriate condition of light and, crucially, given enough space not to be crowded out by stronger growing plants. To maintain this situation indefinitely creates a burden or a pleasure for a gardener, but plants may dominate or be dominated. The change usually involves short-lived plants being replaced by longer lived and then woody plants. This is known as succession and culminates in a relatively stable climax community.

In speaking of evolution, it is too easy to think of organisms 'wanting' to do something – to grow close to the ground, to grow to reach the light, to hide in

Dappled shade allows bluebells to grow amongst grasses at the University of Bristol Botanic Garden.

rocks. These are adaptations that have developed through eons of survival of those that hide, fight or reproduce most effectively; those whose hormones have been most sensitive; and those whose reactions have been fastest, amongst many other attributes. Evolution operates on the variable environmental tolerances conferred by gene diversity in a population. Many plants evade competition by growing in

Growing Constraints

As well as the visible signs of competition, there are some less obvious. Certain plants, and particularly trees, exude compounds from their roots or leaves that inhibit the germination of ground flora in a process known as allelopathy. Particularly relevant in gardens are the defences of *Juglans regia* (Plants for a Future, n.d.) and *Ailanthus altissima*, vigorous and stately trees in a large garden, which in the wild protect their space by making the soil hostile to emerging plants. Parasites debilitate plants by taking nutrients from the host, a function that can be put to use by designers in using yellow rattle to weaken grasses and favour other meadow plants. To be successful, parasites must either keep their hosts alive or become saprophytic – able to continue living on the dead remains of the host. Other organisms may have mutually beneficial effects, such as the symbiotic relationship mycorrhizal fungi have with many trees and other plants, which we will discuss in Chapter 4.

conditions that are not ideal. We see sheets of bluebells under mature trees in spring, but they also grow vigorously in brighter light if the opportunity arises; for instance, in gardens where they are protected from competition from more aggressive plants.

If the requirements for survival are met, competition may determine if an organism will thrive or fail. Human influence on changing the setting is obviously important in gardens, but to maintain a garden in a static condition is to miss opportunities for increasing species diversity. Nowhere is this seen more clearly than in the treatment of lawns. Many of the plants found in pastureland are ones that grow close to the ground as rosettes; others are stoloniferous and send their shoots out sideways instead of upright. In creating lawns, we take advantage of this by sowing grasses that can thrive, growing low to the ground. Other plants that are considered lawn weeds, such as creeping buttercup and moss, benefit from mowing because they compete well without

needing to be tall. On the other hand, when the plants around them grow tall, they are shaded out and compete badly. Living in a constantly mown condition, lawns are perpetually in a juvenile state, never getting a chance to reproduce. In the words of Michael Pollan, 'Lawns are nature purged of sex or death' (1991: p.68). They support very little other life, and are sometimes described as a 'green desert', but they create a rich habitat in the soil, where microorganisms have broken down detritus and fibrous roots have finely penetrated the soil.

Naturalistic Planting

Although we are not attempting to recreate the natural world in our gardens, designers and gardeners interested in creating habitats must start to think about plants as communities, rather than as cossetted individuals, and to understand how these communities are adapted to a specific garden situation. There needs to be an understanding – and a setting of expectations – that such planting combinations are not static but will change over time in much the same way as wild communities (Rainer, 2018). Selecting plants that occur together naturally in a particular habitat is a good starting point for the designer. For example, in a shady garden we can learn from how plants behave in woodland or for a roof garden we can look to the combinations found in exposed situations, such as clifftops.

Looking at how the plants behave in the wild can give clues as to how they will spread. In nature, plants grow through and around each other, some coming to dominance in different seasons and then dying back, others growing tall and shading their neighbours. There may be tens or even hundreds of plants found in one square metre, compared with the relatively tiny number found in a garden (Kingsbury, 2013). However, reproducing or imitating nature is not always the answer; not only is high-density planting costly, but it also requires an in-depth understanding of the relative competitiveness of each plant and knowledge of how they will behave in combination in the specific garden situation. It is often stated that if designers create a dense layer of ground-cover planting, it will reduce the number of weeds; however, this is not necessarily the case. Weeds are

Convolvulus arvensis, Plantago lanceolata, shepherd's purse, ryegrass and other grasses of waste ground naturally intermingled at this field edge.

opportunists and there will always be some that thrive in the shadiest positions under, or in the very centre of, perennials or ornamental grasses.

In Chapter 8, we will introduce a design approach that we called interlacing, which most closely approximates the intermingling seen in nature. A combination of plants is chosen and planted randomly across an area. The percentage of each plant is specified, depending on its competitiveness and its function in the scheme. Piet Oudolf is an exponent of this planting approach. He starts with a matrix of long-lived background plants to which he adds flowering perennials, chosen for colour and structure, and a scattering of ephemeral plants to create dynamism (RHS, 2021c). For example, in a shady woodland scheme, Oudolf might specify roughly 40 per cent ferns, 25 per cent sedges and 35 per cent ground-cover perennials (Spencer, 2020).

Seasonal Succession

Continuity in the sequence of flowering is another important factor to consider when choosing the mix. For a small-scale successional planting scheme, Nigel Dunnett, from the University of Sheffield, suggests using 20 per cent structural grasses and the same percentage of spring-flowering perennials, with 30 per cent of summer- and autumn-flowering perennials that will gradually overshadow the spring flowers as the seasons progress (Heatherington and Sargeant, 2005).

Planting Density

Whether the designer chooses to intermingle or to plant in blocks and drifts, the question of plant density remains. Traditionally, we are taught to use spacings of 30, 40, 50 or even 60cm. Most of the plans in this book are drawn with these approximate spacings. Some nurseries suggest seven or nine perennials per square metre, resulting in more competition between plants. Planting densely allows plants to wind through and support each other as they clamber to reach the light. Kingsbury (2019) has undertaken informal trials over seven years looking at intermingling high-density planting schemes to examine whether one species will ultimately dominate and to see whether weed suppression occurs. His results show that, although some perennials disappeared within two or three years, there was no overall winner. Surprisingly, although the plots were in the same situation and treated similarly, there were different results in each, showing that competition could not be completely predicted.

However, Rosi Rollings, whose research into the attractiveness of perennials to pollinators we will discuss in Chapter 3, suggests that bees might actually prefer blocks of the same flower, rather than an intermingling scheme. When we visited Rollings' Rosybee nursery near Monmouth in July 2021 and interviewed her about her research, she pointed out that for honey bees, in particular, it has to be worthwhile them visiting a plant; there need to be plenty of flowers of that species in full bloom. Her observations indicate that if there is a solitary flowering plant, it is the bumble bees that visit. But even bumble bees prefer ease of access to nectar. As Rollings commented, 'If they can walk from one flower to another, they will'. Ultimately, the choice of density depends on budget and the future management of the garden; approximately six per square metre is suitable for most medium-sized perennials when planting in blocks; any more than this and the plants will grow tall to try to reach the sun and then flop over and need staking.

Another important result from Kingsbury's research to consider when creating habitats in gardens and deciding on planting schemes and densities, is the fact that slower growing perennials and grasses, especially those that start their growth periods later in the year – such as *Miscanthus* and *Panicum* – are quickly outcompeted. In contrast, plants that form a dense mat of rhizomes or with extensive root systems tend to dominate (Kingsbury, 2019).

Biodiversity

It is not difficult to understand that a garden where bare soil and short grass dominate hosts little wildlife. Primary production is the rate at which solar energy is harnessed in photosynthesis and converted into organic compounds: carbohydrates stored in plant tissue, which ultimately nourish all other forms of life. Equally it is clear that a garden with an abundance of healthy plants is undertaking more photosynthesis. Where the vegetation is layered, plants that use varying intensities of light can co-exist, and photosynthesis can take place at every level. It is this process, and the fact that levels of vegetation offer more to the environment spatially, that also promotes an increase in habitats and drives biodiversity. (For more information about how ecological processes are regulated by biological diversity *see* Cardinale *et al.*, 2011). In the words of the writer Barry Lopez: 'Diversity is not a mere characteristic of life . . . [it] is a condition necessary *for* life. Diversity creates the biological tensioning that makes life in general vigorous and sustainable' (Lopez, 2020: p.84).

We have seen how change is inherent in ecological systems. As we will discuss in Chapter 2, assessing the site includes observing what should be left untouched and where opportunities for enhancing biodiversity lie. Some limitations may present possibilities for radical solutions. The sheer volume of products on sale to remove moss from lawns, paths, decks and paving is testament to how easily moss grows, and in the right circumstances – where grass does not thrive amongst the fine roots of beech trees, for instance – moss can make a striking ground cover, creating an atmosphere completely in character with the setting. Lichens are slower to establish and unresponsive to introduction; to retain existing lichens, which confer a sense of longevity, it is important to maintain their existing setting.

A flush of *Anthriscus* and grasses before the oak canopy becomes dense.

Lichens colonizing ageing wood in the clean moist air of Jura, with yellow *Potentilla* naturally interlacing.

Succession

In nature, the landscape is not in stasis, but what we have come to consider as natural is rarely unaffected by human activity, and gardens are a prime example of places where successional changes in vegetation, and consequently animals, may be limited or eliminated entirely. In farming, the modification has been from a dynamic patchwork of vegetation types to a constantly rejuvenated pattern of fields, whether arable or grazed, surrounded, decreasingly, by hedges that are themselves kept in a static juvenile condition. Hedges are now a rich reservoir of habitats. Although they are known to have existed since the Bronze Age, the explosion in the extent of hedgerows came in the late eighteenth and early nineteenth centuries with the Enclosure Acts, when 200,000 miles of hedgerows were planted (Woodland Trust, 2013).

Nature may abhor a vacuum, but in traditional horticultural practice the vacuum is regularly restored. In gardens, we clear patches of ground of all vegetation

Vegetation of heathers, moss, ferns and grasses colonizing the unstable substrate of fallen rocks in North Wales.

from time to time for vegetables, for creating space and for furthering our design aims. Ground that is left bare quickly acquires a cover of ruderals, which we may consider as weeds when we find them objectionable. Seeds may already be in the soil, or they may blow in and find favourable conditions. At this stage, plants that do not compete well with other plants, but which germinate and propagate themselves quickly, flourish and are the ones most often consid ered weeds, albeit easily controlled ones. Field poppy, chickweed and fat hen are all examples of these. Given a bit longer, more tenacious perennial buttercup and brambles will establish themselves, followed perhaps by ash and sycamore seedlings.

Other plants may appear when different circum-stances prevail; this is seen to spectacular effect in tree plantations when felling has taken place: foxglove and willowherb seeds, which have lain dormant for many years, germinate when exposed to the light and create a feast of pollen and nectar for bees and other insects, and a feast for the eyes for humans. The plants persist for a year or two until other plants overwhelm them. When felling persists annually in adjacent areas, insect populations benefit from increasing diversity in the plants that germinate in the new conditions, but the nature of life both in the wild and in humanized land-scapes can be more boom and bust, a situation that can be evened out in gardens with considered planting.

In most temperate environments bare soil is rare, and mature vegetation and longevity result from a minimum of interference. 'Maturity' in gardens is has-tened by planting densely, but large specimens are not necessarily a shortcut, taking longer to establish. Some plants will tend to be out-competed, and the choice is up to the designer to decide to what extent to accept this. In due course, others need to be removed to pre-vent them becoming dominant, maintaining a mixture of young and established habitats, which favour a wide variety of wildlife.

Native and Non-Native Plants

We have seen that change is inherent in ecology. It is a very sterile garden that does not develop and mature but is constantly brought back to base or to bare earth.

Meadowsweet and rosebay willowherb at the woodland edge.

Silver birches are showing signs of failure in SE England, while thriving further north and west.

Good design allows for flexibility, and in dealing with climate change, we must prepare for new circumstances. This is no time to limit our perspective on what vegetation will thrive to benefit animal life, but we should be alert to introductions that could become problematic. The loss of the land bridge between Great Britain and Europe around 10,000 years ago halted the spread of species advancing northwards following the end of the Ice Age. This left us with a relative paucity of native plants and animals, and to limit ourselves to these would be little insurance against massive loss of biodiversity as conditions change.

Climate Change

Designers must consider how the climate crisis might affect planting choices. Plants that thrive now will not necessarily do so in the future; this applies to both natives and non-natives. James Hitchmough (2020) suggests that already *Betula pendula* is struggling in southern England and *Sorbus aucuparia* will soon follow. There are no easy rules, but it is likely that plants growing in the south of Britain will cope with conditions further north, whilst in the south we will need to look to France and southern Europe for ideas of what might be suitable. Hitchmough (2020) likens the conditions in London today to those on the Croatian plateau where the UK native *Corylus avellana* is found in woodland, together with non-natives *Syringa vulgaris* and *Cercis siliquastrum* in more open areas.

If native plant species are not viable, in order to create habitats that may still be able to support native invertebrates, Hitchmough (2020) suggests looking first at regional ecotypes. An ecotype is a genetically distinct variety that cannot be considered to be so dissimilar from the species as to warrant separate classification. It is adapted to particular geographic conditions. If an ecotype is not appropriate – and in gardens this is probably the case – then Hitchmough advises looking first at species from the same genera and, finally, from the same family. For example, *Quercus ilex* could replace *Quercus robur* and *petraea*, and *Salvia nemorosa* and *Euphorbia characias* could prove useful drought-tolerant garden plants.

Cupressus sempervirens, native to southern Europe, is increasingly thriving in rising temperatures in southern England, seen here at the University of Bristol Botanic Garden.

Careful choice of plants, whether native or non-native, and discernment in what is allowed to proliferate, is dynamic, and management must address this. With succession comes increasing complexity and more variety in habitats. Throughout the following chapters, we will examine how we can promote this through creating layers and corridors, and enhancing different settings. While we can introduce suitable plants and trust that they will thrive, animals will only colonize places that meet their needs. In Chapter 10, we will examine how we can manage gardens to promote complexity through encouraging the development of the design, without compromising design intentions.

Design Tips

- Learn from nature.
- Change can be an opportunity.
- Observe seasonal changes.
- Plant with a view to changing temperatures and rainfall.

CHAPTER 2

GATHERING INFORMATION

For any garden design, the first few visits to the site are all about information-gathering, and taking a detailed survey is an essential first step; this can be supplied by a professional company or undertaken by the designer. With a copy of the survey to hand, the site analysis can begin. When designing with habitats in mind, it is worth thinking about both the macro and the micro, observing everything from topography and existing trees down to tiny corners, piles of rubbish and smaller plant combinations.

In this chapter we examine the process of assessing the site with reference to a garden designed for the Royal Society for the Protection of Birds (RSPB), taking the reader through the analysis step by step. We also discuss the importance of observation and how sketching can be a useful aid, before ending with an essential stage of the information-gathering process – creating a brief.

Site Analysis

A good starting point for any site analysis is to look at a garden's strengths and weaknesses, opportunities and threats (SWOT analysis). For human visitors, these include things such as:

- The position of the house, doors and windows.
- Views – good and bad.
- Access restrictions during the build.
- The quality of the soil.
- The aspect.
- Existing attractive features.

However, when considering habitats, the list can be expanded. The table below shows just some of the aspects to consider in these initial stages of the creation of a garden.

Protection During the Build

While assessing the site for its assets and drawbacks and exploring initial design ideas, we need to have another train of thought running alongside: what will be the logistics of the build, crucially access and storage? An assessment is made of what is valuable to preserve, most of which will need physical protection.

Site analysis for designing habitats	
Strengths, weaknesses, opportunities and threats	**Considerations**
The soil structure and pH	The quality of the soil affects the choice of plants. Different habitats may be created in areas of the garden with different soil composition.
Existing trees	Trees are valuable as cover and as food sources. Consideration should be given to retaining existing trees.
The house and boundaries	Can any of the vertical spaces, such as walls and fences, be used for planting or to create other habitats, such as bug and bee niches? Is there an opportunity to create a green or a brown roof?
Existing habitats, both micro and macro	Existing habitats may already be functioning well, e.g. log piles, walls, compost heaps, holes in wood and banks.
Useful plants	Check whether any of the existing plants are beneficial for wildlife and thriving.
Areas of damp/dry and presence of water	Can these be utilized to create different habitats? Is there potential for a pond or a scree garden?
Other microclimates	Rather than attempting to change these areas, can they be exploited or improved?
Materials that can be repurposed	Focus on sustainability. Are any materials particularly suitable for creating microhabitats?
Neighbouring habitats – good or bad	Neighbouring gardens are both an opportunity and a threat. Are there productive habitats outside the garden that can be connected through the design? Note that habitats outside the garden may change.
Access for creatures across boundaries	Ensure that this continues or is introduced in the new design.
The local area	Observe the flora and fauna of the local area. Are there plants that thrive that could be included in the garden or is there wildlife that could be encouraged?
Unwanted plants and wildlife	Unfortunately, some creatures and plants present a threat rather than an opportunity, e.g. rabbits and deer eating new plants, invasive weeds such as Japanese knotweed.
Self-seeded plants – including saplings	A seed bank of wild flowers can be an asset or a threat. Can a self-seeded sapling, such as hazel or holly, become part of the new garden?
Storing materials	Is there space to store materials for reuse? Which materials can safely be repurposed to create new habitats?
Access to other recycled or local materials	Are there any local materials that would be suitable for new habitats?
Timing of the build	How can the build best be timed to ensure the least disruption to wildlife, the best conditions for retained and transplanted plants, and for seeding meadows or planting new trees and shrubs?

Existing trees have root plates, which are not always symmetrical, beyond their canopy line. The extent of the area that needs to be protected should meet the British Standard 5837:2012, *Trees in relation to design, demolition and construction.* (For further information *see* The Arboricultural Association, 2019). The radius of the required protection area is 12 × the diameter of the trunk (at 1.5 m above the ground). The Woodland Trust suggests that the area should be larger for ancient and veteran trees (Gilmartin, 2021). This is a legal require-ment where planning permissions are involved, but the formula should be applied for protection of any exist-ing trees to be retained.

Protection of water bodies and other habitats needs to be similarly rigorous and allow for the movement of wildlife, where applicable. Where disturbance is unavoidable, hand tools will do much less damage than machinery. Protection obviously means avoiding digging, fires, chemical treatment or physical damage to above-ground parts and is clearest when temporary fencing or boarding prevents access. It also precludes storage, which might cause consolidation of the soil. Small sites can create difficulties for access, storage and disposal, but even in a large site, the working area may stray harmfully, just because there appears to be space.

Topsoil is a resource that is frequently removed and replaced with new, which is not necessarily beneficial, as we will discuss in Chapter 4. Turf that is lifted should never leave site as, stacked and covered, it rots to well-textured topsoil. It is worth noting that seeded lawns, and anything else grown from seed, demand the best ground preparation, but the haulage and storage required are negligible. As we will discuss in Chapter 4 with reference to the work of landscape architect Dermot Foley, demolition materials can also be reused on site – imaginatively for wearing courses or crushed for hard core.

Saving materials for reuse makes further demands on storage space, but creates less movement in and out of the site, which may be an advantage where access is difficult. These are considerations that need to be addressed at an early stage because costs can escalate if unexpected demands are made, and the design could be compromised.

The 'As Found' Approach

In the 1950s, the architects Alison and Peter Smithson coined a new term – the 'as found'. This was a response to the post-war landscape of Britain: the poverty, the detritus, the make-do approach, the fragments of materials, the ordinariness of buildings and remnants. The Smithsons explain that they were not only looking to the wider landscape or to the surrounding buildings when thinking about the 'as found', but also to 'those marks that constitute remembrancers in a place and that are to be read through finding out how the exist-ing built fabric of the place had come to be as it was' (Smithson and Smithson, 1990: p.201). It was through this exploration and understanding of a place, this new way of appreciating the prosaic and the mundane, that the Smithsons felt they could 're-energise our inven-tive activity' (1990: p.201).

The concept of the 'as found' is particularly apt in our time of climate change; we need to find ways to create sustainable landscapes that work as much as possible with the processes and materials that are already present on the site. The Smithsons' explora-tions into the built landscape can, for our purposes, be translated into a need to analyse and understand the ecology, habitats, plants and materials already present in a garden and to use this as a starting point for the creative process.

The RSPB Garden

Although this garden was designed for the Royal Society for the Protection of Birds, it was not intended to be a nature reserve; rather it was designed to dem-onstrate to visitors how they might encourage wildlife into their own gardens. The site on the Suffolk/Essex border had been a garden for decades but was aban-doned for a long period, and when we first visited, it was completely overgrown with laurel, bamboo and × *Cuprocyparis leylandii.* There was very little ground cover due to the extremely low light levels beneath this dense canopy of evergreen shrubs.

The house and other buildings on the site were dilapidated, and the intention was to eventually demol-ish them and to create a visitor centre and workshop

All the spoil, topsoil and rocks disturbed during the build were reused on site in this Hebridean garden.

The rocks in the Hebridean garden are now embedded in the new landscape, surrounded by meadow planting.

Site analysis photos and early thoughts about the RSPB garden.

area in their place. We hoped that some of the rubble from demolition could be used as a sub-base, safety permitting. However, only one of the buildings was to be removed at this stage in the process and the visitor centre would be commissioned later. The other building was a danger to the public and was screened with a simple wooden fencing that we planted with climbers.

The survey drawings and photos show parts of the analysis of the site that we undertook over the course of several months. It is useful to be able to observe a garden through the seasons to see what habitats are present and whether they are successful. However, it is unlikely that this will be possible in most cases, and the designer will need to rely on their detailed analysis of the site, information from the client and observation of the sort of plants and wildlife that are thriving in neighbouring gardens and around the local area.

The RSPB site slopes steeply towards the River Stour, and behind the existing buildings there was a bank that needed to be retained to prevent it slipping once the building was removed. The soil was sandier around the buildings and on the top bank, and became darker and more humic towards the river. There was also a boggy area where an underground spring bubbled up, and the lower part of the site flooded at times. The pH varied from 6.1 to 6.8: it was probably acid in places due to leaf fall from the dense shrub cover.

As part of the site analysis it may be useful to call on experts to advise on trees, drainage, ponds and watercourses, for example. An arboricultural assessment was carried out for the RSPB. Some of the trees were deemed unsafe and others were selected to have their canopies raised providing views through the site and to the river. Willows were chosen for re-pollarding. We checked the spot levels for all the trees that were to remain to ensure that the design made no changes to the soil levels in the region of their roots. Other than the trees, there was very little vegetation to retain, except for some of the elders on the bank and sloping areas at the top of the site.

We saved all the logs from the felling of the unsafe birch trees to create log steps and log piles to be placed around the completed garden, and we were able to make use of sweet chestnut branches from another local RSPB site as palings along the boundaries. We also used wood from the fallen and felled trees and from the surrounding area to create benches.

Other considerations included the threats posed by deer and rabbits munching the new plants and the stand of Japanese knotweed that was on a three-year treatment programme, which necessitated that there be minimal digging in that area. Finally, we had to consider how the garden would be managed in the long term; the intention was to use volunteers under the guidance of a full-time employee.

Over the course of our visits, ideas for the design of the garden started to emerge and solidify. We analysed the views into, out of and around the site, and combined this information with access and circulation routes. The sloping site and relatively low budget for such a big project compounded the complications; we needed to provide disabled access to as much of the site as possible, as well as making the compacted gravel paths safe and well drained. Sections and elevations were an essential tool for us when finalizing the design; we used a 'cut and fill' approach to ensure that little waste had to be removed off site.

We also endeavoured to make the best use of the sunny and shady parts of the site and of the damper and drier soils. We had hoped to create a pond in the area of the natural spring but had to revise this and instead construct a deck to cross the boggy area, which we seeded with native wildflowers to cope with damper conditions. We incorporated a varied range of materials to create habitats, such as mud, dust, pine needles, compacted gravel, decaying logs, bee and bug posts, and woven willow and hazel. We also specified a range of regimes for the grass and meadow areas. Analysis and treatment of the existing trees ensured that we were able to create spaces that were open and others where there was cover. Our choice of new trees, suggestions for thinning and pollarding those already on site, and our retention of the ivy stumps in the design, meant that we were able to ensure that the trees in the garden will have a wide age-profile into the future. The final design included new trees, native hedges, large expanses of perennials and grasses, woodland (see Chapter 6), an orchard, woven willow ridges and pollarded willows (see Chapter 4), meadows, a coppiced hazel grove and a vegetable garden.

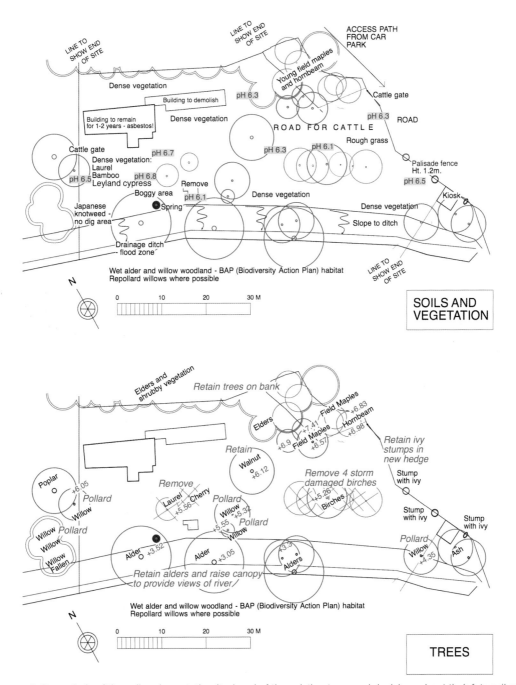

Survey and site analysis of the soil and vegetation (*top*) and of the existing trees and decisions about their future (*bottom*).

View to river

Wet alder and willow woodland BAP habitat

Slope to flooded ditch

Repollard willows to open up ground layer

Deck for access perhaps

Access for cattle
Flat area - main path for people?

Willows grow back after pollarding

Views to river - possibly raise canopies

Keep walnut

View from entrance after removal of birch trees

Plenty of sun for perennials

Flooded ditch- Deck for access

Site analysis photos showing views and thoughts about trees.

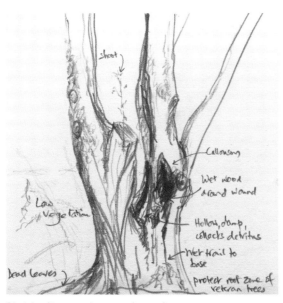

Sketch of tree ecology, made on site.

View of RSPB site from the entrance with the retained birch tree surrounded by an arc of habitat niche posts providing refuges for invertebrates. Benches made from retained timber.

Logs from the site are repurposed as grassy steps.

MARIANNE MAJERUS

Sketch of fallen trees, made on site.

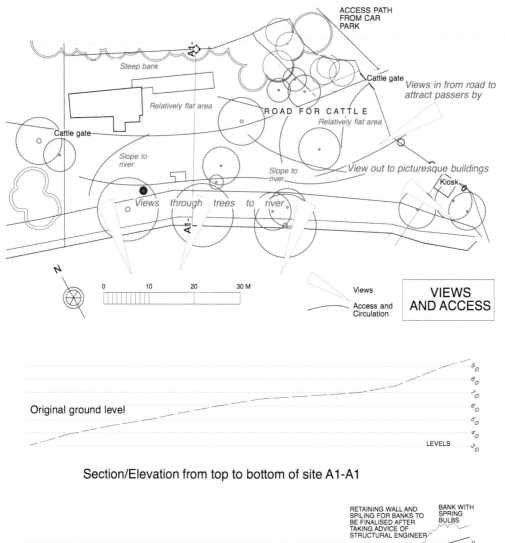

ACCESS PATH FROM CAR PARK

Steep bank

Relatively flat area

Cattle gate

ROAD FOR CATTLE

Relatively flat area

Views in from road to attract passers by

Cattle gate

Slope to river

Slope to river

View out to picturesque buildings

Kiosk

Views through trees to river

N

0   10   20   30 M

Views

Access and Circulation

VIEWS AND ACCESS

Original ground level

90
80
70
60
50
40
30

LEVELS

Section/Elevation from top to bottom of site A1-A1

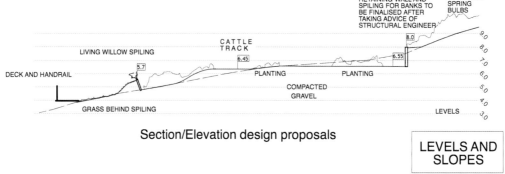

RETAINING WALL AND SPILING FOR BANKS TO BE FINALISED AFTER TAKING ADVICE OF STRUCTURAL ENGINEER

BANK WITH SPRING BULBS

LIVING WILLOW SPILING

CATTLE TRACK

8.0

6.45

6.55

DECK AND HANDRAIL

5.7

PLANTING

PLANTING

COMPACTED GRAVEL

GRASS BEHIND SPILING

90
80
70
60
50
40
30

LEVELS

Section/Elevation design proposals

LEVELS AND SLOPES

Survey and site analysis showing views through the site and possible access routes (*top*). Existing and new elevations through the site down to the river (*bottom*). Note the use of cut-and-fill techniques.

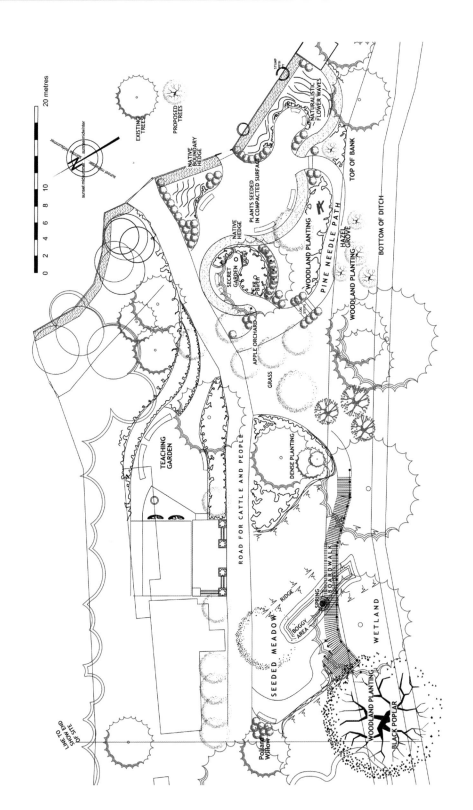

Final plan of the RSPB garden.

During the build, showing the slope down to the flooded river.

The completed garden: the meadow slopes down towards the river and a decking walkway provides access.

Front Gardens

Front gardens might seem unsuited to the creation of wildlife habitats. In cities, in particular, they are often small and overcrowded with the functional requirements and detritus of urban life: hard standing for cars, several bins, meter boxes, bike stores and litter. However, there are also opportunities. If like-minded neighbours can work together, front gardens, with their low fences, can form mini-wildlife corridors. In the information-gathering stage, designers can explore ideas with the residents and identify ways to introduce mini-habitats. Threats such as bin and bike stores can be designed with green roofs, turning them into opportunities, and if it is essential that cars are parked in the garden, then there is the challenge to be creative with permeable paving.

An opportunity to create a habitat in a front garden.

This front lawn has been allowed to grow long and a tapestry of non-native fox-and-cubs has established.
BETH MINDEL-HOLMES

The house walls are a vertical space waiting for planting: climbers on tensioned stainless steel cables can be trained around doors and windows. Houses also provide nesting opportunities. At the site-analysis stage, look carefully to see if there are gaps under the eaves or explore whether the walls are suitable for the installation of swift boxes.

Some roads are lined with trees that provide shade and habitats at the canopy level; these are likely to be radically pruned at intervals but are less likely to be removed completely. The garden may be big enough to include a hedge on the boundary, giving shrub cover at the mid-level.

In most front gardens, mown grass seems rather unnecessary, and if the space is big enough, this is the time to explore whether a wildflower lawn could be introduced. However, this step needs to be carefully thought through; passers-by might see only a patch of weeds rather than an intentional wildlife habitat. Nevertheless, the front garden is an opportunity to demonstrate to the local community how a habitat garden can be a feast for the senses throughout the year.

Observing

Although much design now takes place in the digital environment, at the information gathering stage, the experience of being in the landscape is fundamental. It is helpful to think from a phenomenological perspective: we have a bodily engagement with the site (Tilley, 1994). When exploring a garden, we experience it with all our senses, we come to understand the views and the ways in which we might best move around and through the different spaces. We observe the micro and the macro – the detail and the big picture, both of which inform our subsequent design process.

It is at this stage that a sketchbook is a useful tool to help train our observational skills, rather than relying solely on photos. Even quick sketches encourage us to stop, look, listen and attempt to understand what is around us. Janet Swailes, in her book *Field Sketching*

(2016), explains how photographs capture what is there – perhaps in too much detail – whereas sketches are selective and begin the process of interpreting when you are present on site, rather than remotely back at the computer screen.

As we mention above, it is useful to experience the site over time, to observe changes through the seasons and in different weather conditions. These changes can be captured in photographic form but, again, sketches stimulate the senses and may be more revealing as you observe through pencil and paper, rather than through a screen. When designing habitats it can be especially helpful to observe the landscape beyond the boundaries. For the RSPB site, quick sketches of the meanders of the river, the flood plain, the sculptural forms of the pollarded willows and the fallen trees provided design inspiration but also served as reminders of the very specific habitats that linked with the garden.

A quick sketch of the River Stour below the RSPB garden captures the meanders of the river and the distinctive shapes of the willows.

Creating a Brief

As with any design, drawing up a detailed brief is good practice. Although one of the main aims of the design is to create diverse habitats, the needs and desires of the people who will maintain and enjoy the garden are just as important. The site analysis is the starting point for discussions about what the garden might look like, which creatures it could support and how it will be used by humans and animals. All the usual aspects of a brief need to be considered – a formal or informal aesthetic, requirements for entertaining, relaxation and play, desired and functional features, preferred flowers and colours, features to keep, sun and shade preferences, boundary treatments, preferred views and screening.

It is then important to set expectations and to ask questions to establish the best way in which the human priorities can be merged with the habitat requirements:

- Which creatures would you like to attract or cater for?
- Which creatures are more likely to thrive in this garden in the prevailing conditions?
- What are the implications of creating habitats for these creatures and are there other invertebrates further down the food chain that need to be catered for?
- Are any of the neighbours also supportive of creating habitats or are they likely to be unsupportive?
- How much time is there for maintenance?
- What is the level of expertise, especially in understanding the behaviour of plants?
- What level of dynamism or chance is acceptable?
- What valuable habitats are already on the site?

- How can the garden be made more sustainable?
- What materials and plants can be reused?
- What are the possibilities for water harvesting?

It is only after all these questions have been considered that priorities can be set. It may be that some of the initial ideas of possible habitats are not practical for this particular garden and the people who will live in and visit it. For example, a family that needs a grassy area for ball games may not be able to leave the grass to grow longer. However, this could be a habitat that is introduced as children grow older and mown grass is no longer required. An open pond may be too high maintenance, but a simple water bowl can still support small birds. A perennial border may take up too much space, but a well-chosen shrub and a climber can also provide nectar and shelter.

Throughout the information-gathering stages, creative ideas will be germinating; some designers may have a fairly firm vision of how they are going to approach the design, others may wait until they have all the information before they start. When designing habitats, it is important to keep an open mind, to be open to change and to think from the outset about how the garden might change in the future.

Design Tips

- Start with the 'as found' approach.
- Consider potential views in both directions, e.g. back towards the house and from a seating area.
- Observe the micro and the macro, and take comprehensive photos.
- Set expectations with the client.

CHAPTER 3

APPROACHES TO DESIGN

Although it may seem incongruous to discuss design when creating habitats in gardens, in this and the following chapters we discuss how design concepts, far from being superfluous, are in fact helpful and even necessary. In this chapter, we look at the fundamentals of design and explore some of the principles that have relevance when creating habitats, as well as examining some of the recent research that has been undertaken into the value of different plant species for invertebrates.

Designers have long advocated learning from natural landscapes. They notice the ways in which vegetation layers mingle and understand seasonal succession, while also appreciating senescence. Small details and combinations observed in the local area can inform the design, as can extrapolating from large-scale impressions. Although there are few places completely untouched by humans, the wilder world is still a starting point for designers. Learning how plants behave in communities and about the interconnectedness between flora and fauna helps us to create useful garden habitats.

The aesthetics of the natural world are also important and close observation can inform our designs. There are many scenes that inspire: the intermingling of spring flowers in woodland; grasses interspersed with dots of colour in a meadow; the textures and contrasts of rock and wood; changing colours of a mixed hedgerow and verge through the seasons; the sound of water tumbling over rocks; still reflections in a pool. And yet, as well as seeing beauty in each of these scenes, we can also start to understand the habitats they support, from the shelter and food opportunities of hedgerows and old wood to the reproductive environment of a pond, and the nectar and seeds in a meadow.

These are starting points to inform and enrich our designs.

Allium, *Dianthus* and *Veronica* interlaced with grasses in this design by Piet Oudolf at Bury Court.

The Kaplans' Theory

Environmental psychologists Rachel and Steven Kaplan's (Kaplan and Kaplan, 1989) theory of environmental preferences outlines four criteria that affect people's responses to landscapes: coherence, legibility, complexity and mystery.

Although the Kaplans were conducting their research into preferences for American landscapes, it is easy to think about how we might examine the design of a garden in the light of these criteria:

- Is the garden understandable? Can we make sense of it?
- Are there distinctive elements that help us to find our way around?
- Is it interesting? Does it stimulate the imagination?
- Are there mysteries to be discovered?

It is not only the human response to the garden that can be analysed in this way. As we will show, coherence between different habitats is essential, and animals also need to be able to find their way around and move through the different layers of the garden. In the following chapters, we show how spatial complexity and diversity of planting are essential prerequisites for creating productive habitats. Finally, a sense of mystery can be understood as a need for creatures to have access to hiding places and secrecy. Designing with these four criteria in mind helps to ensure that gardens are places for wild things to thrive, while also being spaces that we can enjoy on many levels.

Design Fundamentals

Once the brief is agreed and the site analysis completed, the process of designing can begin. It is important not to forget traditional design principles in the desire to incorporate as many habitats as possible.

Touching the Ground Lightly

As we suggested in Chapter 2, the 'as found' approach is one that can inform all garden design practice, and when creating habitats, it is particularly important. Many new habitats take time to establish (Gaston *et al.*, 2005) and those on the site may already be serving a useful purpose. When designing, think about how these existing trees, shrubs, log piles, compost heaps and even paving materials can be incorporated in the new garden, preferably with as little disturbance as possible. We will return to this and discuss the possibilities for repurposing and reusing materials in more detail in Chapter 4.

Aesthetics

The habitat brief is all about function, but the aesthetics of design are still important. A garden designer sculpts spaces in three-dimensions and in time. We have suggested looking to nature for inspiration; aesthetically, planting schemes for habitats are perhaps the most likely to relate to those found in the wilder world. Naturalistic techniques are regularly used by designers, and accepted and enjoyed by the public. The work of James Hitchmough and Nigel Dunnett from the University of Sheffield has produced a wealth of research findings into the use of these techniques in public spaces. Other designers, such as Dan Pearson, Piet Oudolf, Tom Stuart-Smith, Sarah Price and the late Beth Chatto, have created naturalistic schemes for gardens. The term naturalistic is used to describe designs that are exaggerations or abstractions of nature. Although this way of designing may not always have the creation of habitats as a main focus, the resulting planting is often beneficial to wildlife. These schemes usually specify single flower-heads (for easily accessible food supplies) rather than doubles, and rely on leaving dead flower-heads and seeds over winter (for shelter and food).

Beauty is also found in the ways that elements combine in nature. This is not restricted to vegetation but also includes the contrasts of topography, of ground, rock, water and sky or the dynamism of moving water and billowing grasses and reeds. However, where nature is the inspiration, it is important not to merely create a pastiche of the natural world. Although gardens support wild things, they are not wild places.

Late summer drifts of grasses at Bury Court designed by Piet Oudolf.

A garden of habitats need not derive its aesthetic from nature at all. Imagination and creativity still have a place. Although the minimalist contemporary garden with large areas of hard landscaping and a limited plant palette is the antithesis of the habitat garden, it is possible to design contemporary spaces that are attractive to wildlife. Animals do not need organic or amorphous design forms to survive but, as we will show in the following chapters, can thrive in designed gardens that are contemporary or traditional, formal or geometric, gritty and urban.

Atmosphere

The atmosphere of a garden is an amorphous thing to pin down; it changes and is created by visitors, both animal and human. Nevertheless, the designer puts in place a framework from which the garden evolves. The mood is influenced by such things as density of planting, choice of plants and materials, colour, light, shade,

Stachys, Erysimum and *Nepeta* seen against the hazel hurdle terraces in the RSPB garden. MARIANNE MAJERUS

Framed views in a rectilinear London garden with lush, layered planting.

In this design by Paul Dracott, the deck path winds between multi-stem trees, hovering over the ground layer – another hidden habitat. PAUL DRACOTT

scent and sound. As we will discuss in later chapters, these elements also affect the habitats we are creating.

Atmosphere is also engendered through feelings of privacy, enclosure and seclusion or sociability and expansiveness. These factors are enhanced through the ways in which the designer uses masses and voids or through the framing of views and the circulation of paths. Again any design decisions will affect both people's perception of the space and the uses that the wildlife can make of it.

Extending

Making use of the borrowed landscape in a design is often difficult in urban situations where it is more likely that unpleasant views need to be screened rather than having attention drawn to them. However, there are times when the designer makes reference to landscape beyond the boundary, framing a view or using the forms and shapes of the topography, buildings or vegetation to inspire the design and layout of the garden.

When designing for wildlife, the corridors between favourable patches of habitat are crucial. If gardens are sealed with walls and fences then some ground-dwelling creatures will not be able to enter or leave. Even when a designer takes account of the borrowed landscape, the boundaries and the house are usually the determining factors in the spatial layout of the garden. In order to create useful habitats, we need

Framed views into the borrowed landscape at Broughton Grange, in this design by Tom Stuart-Smith.

to think beyond the fence and link the design of the planting within the garden with that outside – extending the garden into the wider surroundings. There is no guarantee that this extended landscape will remain unchanged, but it is worth taking the risk, while also planning for change. If there are mature trees in a neighbouring garden, these are a starting point; however, it is sensible to include a young tree in the design just in case, in a few years, the landscape changes. Similarly, make use of climbers coming through the

A Productive Food Garden

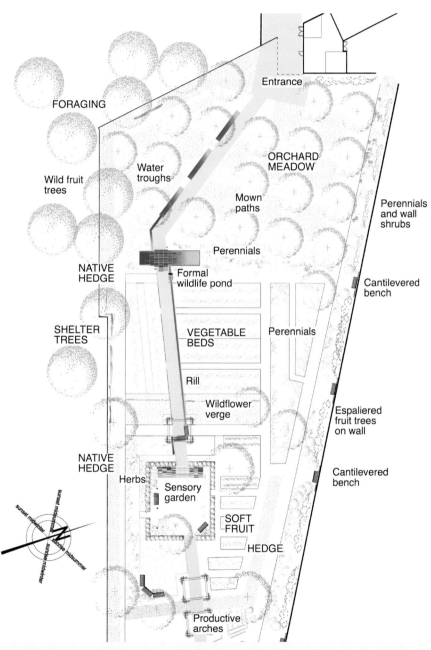

A design for a contemporary productive garden in Dublin, where habitats for pollinators are important.

(Continued)

(Continued)

The brief for the design of this garden on the edge of a city was to demonstrate to visitors how a garden could be a productive resource, whilst also encouraging wildlife. Water, trees and hedges are unifying features in this contemporary design, and paths and mown grass tracks guide the visitor through the different spaces. Each area has its own atmosphere. There are the functional vegetable beds and faintly nostalgic seasonal delights of the orchard and meadow. The sunny boundary wall is a place to sit surrounded by colours and scents, and sensory elements are highlighted in the enclosed herb and sensory garden. These spaces contrast with the wilder foraging woodland and the native hedge that divides the garden from the farmland beyond.

Visitors walk along the path through an orchard beside water troughs and a rill. 'Floating' paving crosses the rectilinear wildlife pond – bringing people close to the water – and the rill continues along the path through vegetable beds, a wildflower verge and under an arch, across a second pond and into a sensory garden edged with lavender and with a long herb bed to one side. The arch is repeated further along the path and planted with climbing berries and vines.

The hedges create wildlife corridors through the gardens and out into the adjacent farmland, and the range of trees and shrubs (some of which were already present) provides opportunities for foraging – hazel, rowan, hawthorn, sloe, rose hips, blackberry and whortleberry. The orchard is planted on a grid with a meadow and mown paths beneath the trees.

Meadows, trees, hedges and water provide a variety of different habitats for insects and birds. Perennial planting is particularly beneficial for pollinating insects such as bees and hoverflies, and the long south-facing walls have built-in solitary bee houses beside benches.

fences from next door, and observe whether there are plants that could self-seed over the boundary or act as pollinators for fruit trees or holly. An extended landscape in a rural situation is often agricultural and of little value to wildlife, but there will be hedges, verges and maybe rough grass forming narrow corridors to link with the more hospitable garden habitats.

Design Specifics

Mass, Void and Form

When designing gardens and landscapes, we create a tension between mass and void. In some cases this entails ensuring that there is a balance between the three-dimensional and the open areas. This allows people to circulate along paths and across lawns and also creates spaces for play and relaxation. These voids are not necessarily beneficial to wildlife but they can

be designed to enable humans to get up close, to observe and to experience the garden with all their senses. But well-planned voids can also be valuable habitats: cracks in paving, spaces under decks, ponds, an unmown lawn and the edges and transitions between voids and masses, all have the potential to attract wildlife.

However, it is the masses that lend themselves to the creation of a wide range of habitats, and it may be that in designing a garden for habitats, the decision is taken to tip the balance between mass and void towards to the former. One of the most important factors that determine whether a garden is attractive to wildlife is the quantity and density of vegetation (Thompson, 2007). Shrubs and trees provide cover and food from the ground plane to the canopy, and densely planted perennials and grasses also add to this mass of vegetation. In choosing shrubs and trees, attention can be paid to the overall form and to the shapes and textures of the leaves. When grouping shrubs, rather than clumping shapes together into a large dark mass, consideration

Formally clipped yews contrast with an exuberant massed planting of *Hydrangea* and *Cornus* in Le Jardin d'Agapanthe, Normandy, designed by Alexandre Thomas.

A tiny habitat demonstrating unity of form and colour, while providing cover and shelter in this urban courtyard designed by Diana Yakeley.

can be given to the contrasting forms and shades of green, thus creating interest and excitement.

Unity

One of the underlying principles of garden design is unity. This is achieved by repeating elements throughout the design, ensuring a limited palette of materials and plants, focusing on creating a particular theme, atmosphere or mood, linking the garden with the house, ensuring one area of the garden flows into the next.

It might appear that in trying to increase diversity for different habitats, unity must take second place; this is not necessarily the case. It is still possible to create a design that focuses on a particular theme or is structured through a succession of repeated shapes. The choice of materials can be determined by those found on site or by restricting materials to those that can contribute to the new habitats.

Repeating the colours and shapes of flowers and foliage also helps to unify the design. There is no reason why a diverse range of perennials in an intermingling planting scheme cannot be designed with a colour scheme in mind. Often the varieties of perennials that are beneficial to wildlife are those with smaller flowers that appear as multi-coloured dots among a unifying background of green foliage. If an exuberant and diverse mix of colours and flower shapes is

Repeating materials, colour and form with the facade 'reflected' on to the cobbled paving, create unity in a garden where habitats for small creatures abound. Designed by Todd Longstaffe-Gowan in collaboration with Amin Taha.

preferred, then the designer can focus on unifying the shapes and forms of the masses and voids, or the excitement of wildly contrasting colours can be framed by the greenery of a hedge or climbers on a trellis.

Bold herbaceous planting amongst mature trees. A simple seat is inserted, creating a link with the framed view of a bridge.

Unity should not be confused with simplicity; more intricate designs encourage greater diversity. This is particularly relevant when designing planting schemes with a complexity that ensures there is beauty and interest for humans throughout the year and also a range of habitats for wildlife. Although only a few of the gardens we design will survive in their present form over decades, it is worth remembering that the climate crisis can lead to unpredictable futures. Trees and shrubs that are adapted to the present conditions may struggle to survive in the future. Therefore, designing with a diverse range of plants becomes imperative (Heatherington, 2021). Indeed, research has shown that not only are complex landscapes good for wildlife, they also benefit humans, increasing a sense of well-being (Cameron et al., 2020).

Sculpting Spaces, Layering and Spatial Division

Thinking of the garden as a temporal, three-dimensional sculpted form can engender creativity, while also ensuring functional requirements are met. During the design process, perspectival and axonometric drawings help to visualize the spaces. It is also useful to map out the areas of mass and void using different colours, so that they can be easily envisaged. This allows the designer to see clearly how the different areas are balanced and whether the spaces left behind – the voids – are also pleasing and comprehensible.

The garden is a maze in which people occupy the voids and the wildlife, broadly speaking, inhabits the masses. In design, we manipulate the layers to create effects, and to provide horizontal and vertical corridors. Spatial complexity is key to the creation of habitats, and throughout this book we refer to layers of vegetation, how they frame spaces, how they benefit wildlife and how they change through the season. Vegetation layers are conventionally divided into canopy, scrub layer and field layer, but we have adopted a finer grained vocabulary for describing them as they can be used in gardens (see table below).

An installation by artist Sarah Sze, linking urban construction with nature and complementing the planting layers on the Highline, New York City, 2012.

Layers in ecology and design			
Ecological	**In design**	**Examples**	**Visual framing**
Canopy layer	Tree layer Canopy layer	Tall mature trees – *Tilia cordata*, *Alnus glutinosa*, *Davidia involucrata*. In small gardens *Sorbus*, *Malus* spp., *Prunus padus* and similar may form the canopy layer	Visibility beneath this layer
Scrub layer/ understorey	Transitional layer	Multi-stemmed trees and climbers – hazels, *Amelanchier*, honeysuckle, ivy, *Crataegus*, *Viburnum opulus*	These are the layers that limit permeability, and may act as screens, barriers or filters
	Hedges/mid and upper shrub layer	*Pittosporum*, *Cornus sanguinea*, *Hippophae rhamnoides*, *Cotoneaster lacteus*, *Stipa gigantea*	
	Shrub and tall herbaceous layer	*Rosa glauca*, *Hebe*, *Eupatorium maculatum* 'Atropurpureum', *Verbena bonariensis*, *Digitalis*, *Dipsacus fullonum*	Visibility over the top of these layers
Field layer	Small shrubs Grasses, ferns and low herbaceous Ground-cover layers	Lavender, *Caryopteris*, *Luzula*, *Molinia* 'Edith Dudszus', *Geranium* 'Rozanne', *Deschampsia caespitosa*, *Vinca*, *Epimedium*	
Ground layer	Mosses, lichens and ground-hugging plants. Underground	Mown grass, wild strawberries, ivy, *Acaena*, *Ajuga reptans*, bulbs, corms, fungi	Layer underfoot

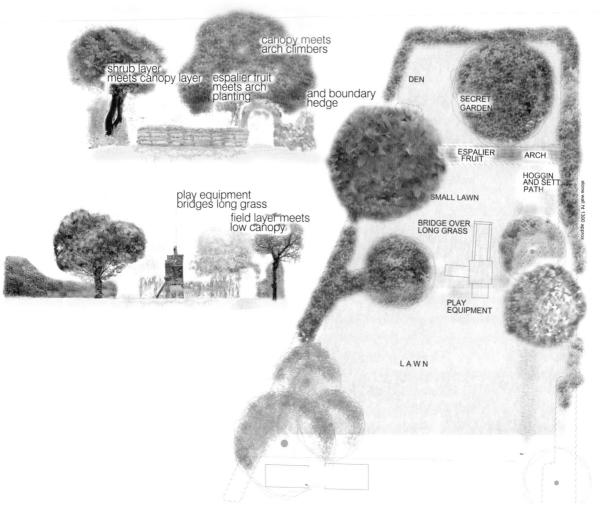

canopy meets
arch climbers

shrub layer
meets canopy layer

espalier fruit
meets arch
planting

and boundary
hedge

DEN

SECRET
GARDEN

ESPALIER
FRUIT

ARCH

HOGGIN
AND SETT
PATH

SMALL LAWN

play equipment
bridges long grass

field layer meets
low canopy

BRIDGE OVER
LONG GRASS

PLAY
EQUIPMENT

stone wall ht 1300 approx.

LAWN

A family garden where trees, lawn, play, meadow and habitats co-exist through layers.

Siting, Circulation and Access

As with any garden, designers need to consider the issues of siting, circulation and access. When designing habitats, these have a twofold importance; the human and animal visitors have specific requirements, and it is necessary to consider how these requirements overlap or come into conflict. In order to enjoy the wildlife, people need to be able to experience it at close quarters and to have places where they can watch from a distance. The views from the house are of equal importance and it might be suitable to site particular habitats, such as a pond or water bowl, so that it is visible from a window. However, the requirements of the habitat must come first. Many features, such as nest boxes and bee houses, have specific needs – there is no point in siting something in a position where it will not thrive or may even fail completely. The maxim 'right plant, right place' is more important than ever in order for plants to provide the best food and shelter, and creatures need to be safely hidden from predators and humans alike.

Subtle dense planting, informal setts, a formally asymmetric design. The siting of the water bowl draws the eye and highlights the design elements. The Sunken Garden in Dedemsvaart, Netherlands, was designed by Mien Ruys in 1960 and restored in 1996.

Where the size of the garden permits, designers can create a sequence of spaces that lead from one to another, with paths and open areas allowing access. Even a small garden can be designed so that its secrets are revealed as the eye travels around the space. This creates a sense of revelation for the visitor, but also has the benefit of providing spaces for wildlife to be relatively undisturbed and hidden.

Some habitats, such as compost heaps and log piles, are usually sited as far away as possible from the main areas of the garden and may be hidden by trellis or dense planting, benefiting both humans and animals.

In a large garden, it is possible to create areas that can remain fairly undisturbed, but often a balance must be reached between the desires of the people using the garden and the needs of the wildlife. The designer has to explain the reasons for siting a habitat in a particular area and to set expectations about what can be achieved.

Choosing Plants

Discussions about the merits of native and non-native plants in wildlife gardens can sometimes be heated and there are various research projects that address this. Two are discussed here: The Royal Horticultural Society's (RHS) *Plants for Bugs* project (2021b) and the work of Rosi Rollings (2019) and Dave Goulson, from the University of Sussex (Rollings and Goulson, 2019).

The RHS's research (2021b) recorded the numbers of plant-dwelling invertebrates, ground-active invertebrates and pollinators over four years on thirty-six plots and concluded that, in a garden situation, native plants are important but non-natives still have a role to play. Overall they found that the greater the number of flowers and the denser the vegetation, the greater the abundance of invertebrates.

When it comes to providing habitats for plant-dwelling invertebrates, native plants performed best, with other northern hemisphere plants (termed near-

Contemporary lush planting layers providing cover and food for wildlife.

natives by the RHS) only slightly less successful (2021b). Abundance of insects was related to canopy cover in every plant group. Plants from the southern hemisphere (termed exotics by the RHS) also contributed to the habitats but supported around 20 per cent fewer species than native plants (Salisbury *et al.*, 2017). The research also showed that ground-active invertebrates were more abundant on native and near-native groups but, again, the exotics, particularly evergreens, could not be ignored, as they provided valuable shelter in winter (Salisbury *et al.*, 2020).

The RHS study recorded pollinators, such as hoverflies, bumble bees, solitary bees and honey bees, in greater numbers on native and northern hemisphere plant groups but also noted that exotics extended the planting season and added to the diversity of flowers available through the year (Salisbury *et al.*, 2015). Rollings and Goulson (2019) agree that native plants attract a greater diversity of pollinators but noted that there was no difference in the overall numbers of insects visiting the plant, irrespective of whether it was native or non-native. Very few of their trial plants fall into the RHS category of exotic. Their findings confirm that non-natives fill a flowering gap at the beginning and end of the year, and in these weeks they attract more insects than native species. Plants studied included early flowerers, *Erysimum* 'Bowles Mauve',

Nepeta mussinii and *Centaurea montana* and the late-flowering *Aster novi-belgii* (Rollings, 2019).

Rollings and Goulson also sound a word of caution; experiments on trial plots differ from gardens with their myriad of plant combinations, soils and microclimates. Goulson makes a further point about lists of pollinator-friendly plants, pointing out that there are many differences and contradictions, and there has been little research into the performance of different varieties and cultivars within a species (Goulson, 2020).

One popular garden plant that has been studied is lavender; researchers at the University of Sussex found that the varieties of *Lavendula × intermedia* were more attractive to pollinators than the *L. angustifolia* and *L. stoechas* varieties (Garbuzov and Ratnieks, 2014). However, they could not explain this difference. There was no evidence that the attractiveness was due to colour, flowering duration or the length of the corolla tube. Rollings' (2019) research supports these findings: *L.* 'Edelweiss' and *L.* 'Grosso' are two of her top-scoring plants for attracting bumble bees.

So how can designers specify plants for creating garden habitats? A good place to start is to refer to the RHS *Plants for Pollinators* (2021d) lists covering wildflowers, garden plants and plants from around the world. Choose from a diverse palette of native and northern hemisphere, and add some carefully selected southern hemisphere species to extend the season and to provide evergreen cover. Gardens must appeal to their human owners and visitors, and specifying mainly native plants, especially in urban gardens, may not be acceptable. Experiment with cultivars of native and northern hemisphere species, especially those with single, rather than double or multiple, flower heads. *Centaurea nigra* and *C. scabiosa* are both native to the UK, whereas *C. montana* is from southern Europe. Rollings' (2019) research shows that the latter is a useful pollinator in the early weeks of the year when there are few natives flowering, and there are many attractive single-flowered cultivars of this species.

We also need to take account of research findings, both about the effects of climate change, as we discussed in Chapter 1, and about the benefits of different species for wildlife. Perhaps the most important thing to remember is that the density of planting and sheer mass of foliage increases the numbers of invertebrates both living in and visiting the garden.

Trees in Gardens

In a new garden, where there is no existing vegetation, the choice of one or more trees is critical. Trees are likely to form the largest single mass of vegetation when mature and their attributes influence much of the garden setting and the wildlife value. Single trees, in particular, should be chosen for a variety of qualities, with food and shelter for animals in mind, as well as the importance they hold for humans.

Early morning sun through mature multi-stem trees. WILLIAM MARTIN

Trees for habitat design				
Species and origin	Size, form, density and growth rate	Conditions and effects	Design attributes	Attributes for wildlife
Acer campestre Native	Fast growth, up to 8m. Open, rounded head, tolerant of pruning.	Widely tolerant of soil and temperature, casts light shade.	Useful adaptable small tree, attractive yellow autumn colour.	Supports caterpillars and aphids and all their predators.
Amelanchier lamarckii North America	Fast growing to 10m. Good as a multi-stem. Light, broad crown, responds to pruning, shaping and thinning, though seldom necessary.	Tolerant of a range of soils, low temperature and some shade. Casts little shade and does not dominate.	Covered in white blossom in spring, small red fruits in summer. Leaves unfold flushed bronze, turn to green, then scarlet/orange in autumn.	Nectar and pollen for bees and other pollinators, berries attract birds.
Arbutus × andrachnoides S Europe and SW Ireland	Best grown as multi-stem. Canopy evergreen and dense. Can be thinned but pruning damages form.	Hardy in all but coldest areas. Tolerates some lime. Creates dense shelter and heavy shade.	Peeling red-brown bark, sculptural branches. Flowers and fruits often seen together in spring.	'Strawberry' fruits held through winter. Nectar and pollen for insects, fruits for birds and bats. Rough bark and dense foliage for cover.
Davidia involucrata China	Slow growing, ultimately can reach 20m. Open, rounded head.	Tolerates cold to –10°C. Thrives in deep, rich, neutral loam.	Spectacular 'handkerchief' bracts in May on mature trees. Good yellow autumn colour. Dramatic specimen given space.	Berries attract birds in winter.
Ilex aquifolium Native	Slow growing, ultimately to 20m and more. Dense, upright evergreen, responds well to pruning and training.	Tolerates cold and drought. Creates dense shade and dry soil conditions.	Distinctive handsome dark green leaves. Bright berries in winter.	Flowers attract pollinators, berries attract birds. Good cover for roosting and nesting birds.
Malus 'Evereste' Cultivar	Small tree to 7m, fast-maturing. Broad, dense crown.	Hardy to –15°C. Open canopy casting light shade.	Copious white blossom in spring, orange red fruits in autumn, useful tree for small gardens.	Pollen and nectar for insects, fruit for birds and small mammals, and leaves eaten by caterpillars of moths and butterflies.
Pittosporum tenuifolium New Zealand	Evergreen tree, can reach 8–10m. Narrow crown, light cover.	Tolerates all soils except wet. Hardy in Ireland and southern England. Receptive to training and pruning.	Tiny purple blossoms in May, highly scented in the evening. Pale undulating leaves.	Flower attractive to bees. Copious seeds attractive to birds, particularly long tailed tits. Foliage provides good cover.

(Continued)

(Continued)

Species and origin	Size, form, density and growth rate	Conditions and effects	Design attributes	Attributes for wildlife
Sambucus nigra Native	Small, fast-growing tree, to 7m. Dense, broad, tangled crown.	Tolerates wide range of conditions. Receptive to pruning and coppicing.	Umbels of highly scented cream flowers.	Open, flat flowers good for short-tongued insects, berries for birds.
Sorbus torminalis Native becoming scarce but may be useful in a changing climate (Hitchmough, 2020)	10m in 20 years; ultimately to 25m. Open canopy, irregular spreading form.	Tolerates cold, and most soils. Casts light shade.	Good autumn colour, crimson berries.	Pollen and nectar for insects, berries for birds, leaves eaten by some moth caterpillars.

Sources: *The Gardener's Illustrated Encyclopedia of Trees and Shrubs* (Davis, 1987); *Trees in Britain, Europe and North America* (Phillips, 1978); Woodland Trust (Woodland Trust, n.d.-c).

Native trees are reliably valuable to wildlife, though they may not provide the most pollen or nectar, and their season may be short. The choice of trees for gardens is so large that it is useful to make an analysis of the attributes of a selection.

Trees are key to the character of a garden. Their selection is one of the earliest planting decisions designers make because they influence everything else in the place we are creating. In nature, trees would tend be the last plants to establish and influence the lower layers. Our choices of trees, or their absence, will determine many of the microclimates of the garden and the success or failure of other planting.

Design Tips

- Consider three dimensions and time from the outset.
- Spatial complexity is key to the creation of habitats.
- Think about how masses and voids can support habitats and enhance people's experiences; ensure the voids are harmonious shapes for humans to occupy.
- Extending the design to include the borrowed landscape can enhance wildlife corridors.

CHAPTER 4

BUILDING BLOCKS

In this chapter, we look under the ground to examine the role soil plays in the design of a garden. We then turn our attention to the hard landscaping elements that share the ground, middle and transition layers with planting, and consider how these elements can work together to create diverse habitats before finally returning to the idea of the 'as found' and exploring some examples of repurposed and recycled materials.

Under the Ground

Soils

It is fundamental to design to understand the soil you are working with. Plants that thrive are visually more pleasing; and to wildlife, more productive of all the things that they are interested in. While many garden plants are not particularly fussy about the range of soils commonly found in established gardens, some need particular soil conditions, just as they need to be suited with respect to shade and competition.

The organic components of soil draw many wild creatures for food, moisture and shelter. The frequently recommended 'well-drained soil with good moisture retention, pH 6.5–7' beloved of gardening books is hard to come by and, actually, could result in a garden restricted in character. The designer can use the limitations of the soil in creating a garden rooted to its surroundings. The genius of the place is not always visible.

In established gardens, we are unlikely to come across soils that are entirely inorganic, but in situations where soil has not been subject to biological processes, it may consist only of the mineral components. Depending on what those minerals are, they may or may not support the growth of plants in the short term, but over time further activity is necessary to keep the soil 'open' and aerated with the capacity to retain water and dissolved nutrients. Mature topsoil contains a range of organic materials, which is maintained by allowing more organic matter to accumulate and to be broken down in it. Healthy soil is a significant carbon sink – an important reason to look after it.

Progress has been made in recent years in manufactured soils, created from a combination of mineral waste and organic material. They result in a product that is consistent and can meet specific requirements for the plants grown. In small quantities they can be made on site, obviating the need for transport and storage, neither of which favour the health of the soil. In gardens, a typical mix would be: broken-up subsoil, which determines the texture; compost, which provides nutrients and humic conditioner; and shredded bark, aiding nutrient retention without releasing significant amounts of carbon dioxide. Research at Plymouth University has trialled various sources of carbon, including biochar, which is carbonized organic material, such as charcoal. These increase the sustainability of manufactured soils by aiding the retention of nitrogen necessary for plant nutrition and contributing to carbon sequestration (Schofield et al., 2019).

Green roofs are a special case, requiring specialized soils, of varying fertility, and recent research at WRAP (the Waste Resources and Action Programme) has trialled the use of commercially produced PAS100 compost with a number of mineral waste materials (WRAP, 2021). We mention green roof substrates below and will discuss green roofs more generally in Chapter 9.

The soils found in new developments of all kinds are usually lacking in topsoil, and the subsoil that is left is devoid of life. Buying in new topsoil can be successful if the designer can vouch for the source and the quality. The standard for topsoil bought and sold is BS:3882 (2015), but there is no substitute for inspecting it before it is ordered, and again before it is unloaded.

We would be in a rather bleak place without trees, as is well recognized. Although not every environment is suitable for trees, most temperate to tropical regions have that potential. In some situations, such as new developments, it is necessary to create the conditions that support their long-term growth. New street trees also need care in the provision of suitable soil. Soil that has lain under pavements and roads is unlikely to contain anything useful for plant uptake, and neither does the compacted subsoil left after development has taken place.

Mycorrhiza

Plants create their own nutrients – sugars from carbon dioxide and water, and mineral compounds from solutes in the soil, which they build into the complex compounds required for their structure and functions. Like humans, fungi are unable to build their own nutrients and they rely, ultimately, on plants to supply them. The relationship may be saprophytic or parasitic, or symbiotic where two or more organisms participate to their mutual benefit. A fungus–plant symbiotic association, which is particularly important in plant nutrition, exists between many plant species and the broad range of mycorrhizal fungi. A mycorrhizal relationship is one in which the fine hyphae of a fungus lives on, or in, the fine roots of a plant. Healthy soils contain the fungi that participate in this process, but in new and inorganic soils, it may be beneficial to introduce them.

Trees are particularly known to benefit from mycorrhiza. Sugars created by the plant in photosynthesis are available for take up by the fungus, which itself supplies nutrients that it has derived from breaking down other plant material, for the benefit of its mycorrhizal partner. These fungal networks are extensive and can connect with many trees. In some cases, the fungus becomes obvious to us – chanterelles, for instance, are the above-ground manifestation of their exclusive mycorrhizal relationship with beech trees.

While most mature soils found in gardens contain the cocktail of fungi that will associate with many plants, inorganic soils or subsoil have not built up the soil flora that contains them. In this situation it may be beneficial to apply a commercial mycorrhizal fungus solution; though well-rotted compost, if available, is likely to have the same effect.

Hard Landscaping Elements

As we show throughout this book, the gardens that are the most densely planted are best for wildlife. However, when designing gardens for people, we need to include areas of hard landscaping and to consider how these can be adapted as habitats. In this section we explore how hard landscaping elements form the building blocks for the spatial structure and system of layers within the garden.

Designs that encourage plants to merge with, and into, paved areas and walls, or to self-seed in gravel, are more likely to have an informal aesthetic. But geometry and formality can be introduced in the form of sweeping curves, rectilinear raised beds and contemporary arches and screens. A diagonal design can create possibilities for including larger planting beds, and more abstract and unusual shapes lend themselves to the use of materials such as crazy paving.

The design detail of these curves of hand-made bricks also helps to retain the compacted gravel path. Vegetation and small branches blur the transition between the soft and hard landscaping.

Local materials are used for this informal path and gaps between the rocks are colonized with low-growing *Dymondia*, a native to South Africa where this photo was taken.

Surfaces – the Ground Layer

Ground layers, whether hard or soft, have the potential to contribute to habitats. The rougher and more varied the surfaces included in the garden, the more potential for exploitation by small plants and animals. The texture of the ground surface, and consistency beneath it, determine its accessibility to soil inhabitants. Leaving dying plant material on the soil over winter creates another valuable habitat. Many grasses, particularly when grown *en masse*, make mats of dense vegetation, dry insulation and seeds for food. Some plants, such as *Ceratostigma plumbaginoides*, die back more elegantly than others and if they do so

while offering protection for small creatures, and even food, so much the better. Rotting wood, rubble and plant debris are valuable in providing homes for small mammals and invertebrates, and are also substrates on which plants can grow. Gravel, pebbles and rock are places to shelter and for plants to self-seed into. They are useful materials for the edges of ponds and as transitions between areas – perhaps when moving from a more formal to an informal space.

There are some areas of the garden where hard surfaces are necessary, but even lichens have difficulty getting a grip on smooth, sawn paving. Leaving permeable gaps between paving stones creates possibilities. Cracks and crevices can be planted with tough, low-growing species, and larger planting gaps can be designed in bigger expanses of hard landscaping. *Erigeron karvinskianus* and *Campanula poscharskyana* both thrive in cracks in surfaces, walls and steps. *Aubretia* and single-bloomed varieties of *Dianthus* are also possibilities, and in damp shade *Soleirolia soleirolii* adds a ground layer of vivid green.

Paving can be laid in a chequerboard design in a lawn or as stepping stones, rather than a solid path. Edges of the patio and paths can be designed to 'bleed'

The risers of the Lutyens steps at Great Dixter are a mass of small ferns, *Alchemilla* and *Soleirolia soleirolii*.

into the planting beds or areas of longer grass, creating an important transition or edge habitat. If a parking area is required in a front garden, this can be adapted to ensure that it meets the SuDS (sustainable drainage systems) requirements, while also providing shelter for small creatures. The solution might be as simple as including two strips of paving to drive on to, surrounded by gravel or another permeable surface. Or for a contemporary aesthetic, a steel mesh can be installed over a recessed area, which is planted with low-growing species.

If a large paved area is a non-negotiable requirement for the garden, planters can create smaller habitats near the house. Blueberries, which need acid soil, are a rewarding plant to grow in pots. They have pretty blossom – for nectar lovers – wonderful autumn colour and, of course, fruit that can be shared with blackbirds and robins. In the right conditions, decking can be an asset providing shelter and corridors for creatures – logs, dried grass and bits of twigs could be stored in the space beneath – at the same time as offering solutions to problems such as drainage, level changes and costs. Alternatively, draining the patio or terrace into areas of planting gives an opportunity for introducing different plants that cope with periods of damp.

An Exposed Roof Garden

Gilles Clément created his Jardin du Tiers-Paysage on the roof of the World War II German submarine base in Saint-Nazaire, France, as part of a development project to repurpose the brutalist concrete structure, with its disturbing memories, as a cultural centre for tourism and the arts (Heatherington, 2021). A section of the extensive concrete roof is divided into ten compartments, each with thick walls on two sides but completely exposed to the Atlantic winds. The walls are a reminder of the site's history: the original construction of the roof was designed to withstand allied bombing raids.

The design of a roof garden is necessarily experimental; it is at the mercy of the weather, and plants that thrive elsewhere may easily fail as salt winds sweep across new growth. Clément embraces the element of chance; he allows these compartmental gardens to develop and change over time with only minimal maintenance. There is a shallow layer of substrate and pebbles retained at each end by reclaimed metal beams. Gradually, a sparse mosaic of discrete habitats is evolving. Originally, the garden was planted with low-growing sedums and grasses. These plants are found along the maritime coast and were thought likely to cope with the adverse conditions. However, after more than ten years, euphorbias have started to predominate and, although in other parts of the site stonecrops have colonized areas of concrete, in the garden they have declined in number.

(Continued)

(Continued)

Grasses and *Euphorbias* colonize the roof garden designed by Gilles Clément at St Nazaire in France.

Clément's garden demonstrates how habitats can be created in the most adverse conditions, and that embracing an element of chance can be applied equally well to domestic situations. It is worth noting that, far from being valueless, brownfield sites are important for many invertebrates because of their open mosaic habitats (Buglife, n.d.-b). These, often discrete, habitats can vary depending on the pioneer species that establish on the varied substrates found in derelict post-industrial landscapes. Although our gardens are unlikely to attract rare flora and fauna (Thompson, 2007), it is possible to create scree and gravel areas with a more open habitat to increase diversity. This approach can be applied to roof gardens, as we will discuss in Chapter 9.

Topography, Steps, Retaining Walls and Raised Beds – the Middle Layers

Different levels in a garden result in a range of conditions and microclimates for plants and also for habitat creation. Walls and mounds offer shelter from adverse weather conditions and places for creatures to hide and even hibernate. It is usually wise to work with the existing topography on site and to use the cut and fill method when designing flat areas in a sloping site. Drier, exposed mounds can be created from the spoil left when constructing a pond, and boggy areas are naturally found in dips and valleys.

Creating mounded, sloping beds around a seating area can also contribute to the atmosphere of the garden. If these are planted with perennials and

A contemporary design by Screen4 at the Westonbirt International Festival of Gardens 2003 uses gabions filled with logs and flint to create retaining walls and vertical structures.

grasses, they create semi-transparent, dynamic layers of colour, scent and movement that reach above the heads of seated visitors, thereby extending the field layer into the mid and upper shrub layers of the garden.

Retaining walls, raised beds and steps accommodate changes in level and also contribute to a mid-level layer in the structure. When designing layers with retaining walls, it is important to consider the balance of heights and the scale, as well as using materials to unify the space. The choice of materials is important to maximize the benefit for wildlife. Well-maintained rendered walls may add a basking surface to a habitat, but brick, stone and wood weather attractively and all have the potential to shelter creatures in the cracks and crevices, and to support the growth of small plants, mosses and lichens. These materials are suitable for both traditional and contemporary designs and can be fashioned into geometric shapes or sweeping curves. Gabions are a less obvious material in a garden but make interesting habitats and can be filled with discarded or recycled materials from the site. A more aesthetic appearance is achieved by using pebbles, tiles or slate as a front and top face and hiding the rubble filling behind.

Raised areas and mounds can also be constructed of substrates that are not present in other areas of the garden and, therefore, offer the possibility of introducing a greater diversity of plants. A common example is to incorporate free-draining materials to enable plants that dislike heavy clay to establish.

Living Willow Spiling

Living willow can be used creatively to introduce structural and playful elements into a garden, while also being mindful of shelter habitats. It lends itself to the design of hedges, dens, play houses, tunnels and arches.

In this design for the RSPB, living willow spiling is used to retain a ridge of meadow planting and forms a boundary between an area of woodland and the open grassy meadow. The living spiling posts are driven into the ground at a 20-degree angle and the willow withies are woven between the posts to create the retaining structure.

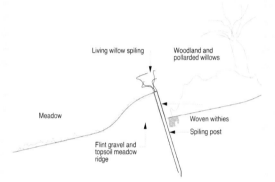

Construction detail for the living willow spiling and meadow ridge at the RSPB garden.

Weaving in progress at the RSPB garden with a pollarded willow in the foreground.

The ridge is built up of flint gravel mixed with topsoil above a drainage layer of clean, crushed brick. It is seeded with a mix of native flowers and grasses that provide some low cover but respond well to mowing every few weeks. Included in the mix are *Galium verum*, *Leontodon hispidus*, *Prunella vulgaris*, *Trifolium pratense*, *Ranunculus acris*, *Agrostis capillaris*, *Festuca rubra* and *Cynosurus cristatus*.

Within a few months, the willow posts start to sprout and quickly grow to hedge height, framing the woodland where existing old willows are pollarded. Pollarding ensures that the willows do not get too large and create dense shadow over the planting beneath, while also retaining the gnarled trunks – another shelter habitat for small invertebrates.

This abstract woven gate at Liseberg Amusement Park in Sweden is designed by 02landskap.

Pergolas, Screens, Arches and Obelisks – the Transition Layer

Finally, we consider features that create divisions and add height to the design, extending between the mid and canopy layers of the garden. Pergolas, screens, arches and even obelisks all fulfil this purpose and support a wide range of climbing plants to provide shelter and food for invertebrates, pollinators and birds. Siting these features in order to benefit the wildlife is important, but they are also attractive to human visitors, dividing the space and drawing the eye around the garden, acting as focal points or providing a seating area in dappled shade. The pergola walkway at the Jardin d'Agapanthe, designed by Alexandre Thomas (shown at the beginning of this chapter), demonstrates how a simple structure of rusting metal can be designed to bridge the layers from field, through tall shrub to create a dense transitional layer, while also drawing the visitor through the garden from shade to light, enclosed to open.

The choice of plants enhances the value of these habitats but the materials can also contribute. Woven willow and hazel are both suitable for smaller obelisks and arches; and for pergolas, a mix of wood and brick or stone can offer possibilities for the smallest of invertebrates to hide from predators or to overwinter.

Vertical accents of *Digitalis ferruginea* against a tall screen of curved Cor-ten framing a naturalistic planting scheme in this city garden. The rusty colour of the foxgloves creates an element of unity and is attractive to bees.

However, for the designer, these vertical elements open up creative opportunities. They can be contemporary or traditional, formal or rustic, quirky or precise – the wildlife does not mind as long as they support a range of climbing plants providing shelter, berries and nectar.

This contemporary pergola in a design by Paul Dracott is set amongst dramatic perennial planting chosen to attract butterflies. PAUL DRACOTT

Greening the House and Boundaries

In small gardens, a large element of the total surface area may be in the vertical surfaces – the fences, trellises and walls, including buildings. These present a large canvas on which to advance the habitat potential of a garden. In many cases, being high up can protect small animals from predation. While cats can climb along walls, they cannot usually climb up them, and halfway up a well-covered wall can be a safe place for nesting birds. Shelter and feeding opportunities abound in climbing plants. However, one of the most important things to remember when designing boundaries is to allow access for creatures, such as hedgehogs, to roam between gardens.

The benefits of greening walls to humans are climate amelioration, both outside and within house

Virginia creeper gradually ascends the rough stone surface of this building designed by Amin Taha, providing shelter. It is planted in small gaps at ground level.

walls, and the cooling effect of shade and evaporation, as well as the beauty and scent that we look to plants to provide.

Planting for Vertical Surfaces

Care must be taken to match the plants to the type of support available. They may be twiners, which need something slender and set away from the wall to climb, leaving a good gap behind for small creatures – honeysuckle, *Trachelospermum jasminoides* and *Passiflora caerula* are good examples and provide pollen and nectar. Clingers attach themselves to a wall, stone, brick or render, rarely to timber, never to plastic, and may become dense – useful for shelter. *Clematis* and the climbing perennial, everlasting sweet peas, are specialized twiners: it is their petioles and specialized leaves, respectively, that curl around supports. *Hydrangea anomala* subsp. *petiolaris*. Var clings and produces flat heads of fluffy flowers loved by short-tongued insects. Clingers such as ivy would naturally

grow up trees as the rough bark gives purchase. Finally, there are rompers that lean in the expectation of finding something to help them up, and these are the ones that need tying in to stop them swamping other plants, the only time when timber trellis may come in useful. Rompers often provide less shelter but more flowers and food – single-flowered rambling roses will romp but flop with nothing to climb over.

Shrubs that will grow against walls tend to give the best shelter – especially evergreen ones like *Garrya elliptica*, *Pyracantha*, *Mahonia* spp. and *Ceanothus* spp.. Winter-flowering wall shrubs also provide valuable food for bumble bees braving the odd warm day in winter. Sunny, sheltered spots against walls benefit plants such as *Clematis cirrhosa* var. *balearica* and *Acacia dealbata*, as well as warming the bees intrepidly venturing out.

Walls

Of the many forms of walls, each can give rise to characteristic mini-environments. Drystone walls contain a labyrinth of crevices, ideal for regulating the temperature of cold-blooded animals and the variations in humidity. In the sun, the face of the wall and its outer crevices can be hot or cold, depending on the weather. Within the wall the temperature is buffered, while a north-facing side experiences temperature swings less in the course of the day than the south-facing side.

A brick or rendered wall absorbs and conducts heat to its interior, which is then released overnight, moderating the ambient temperature of the air. It also provides the substrate that clinging climbers can grip most effectively. Ivy, *Parthenocissus*, *Euonymus* and *Pileostegia* use this method to climb and create the densest cover close to the wall surface.

On house walls, it may not be advisable to use climbers that cling, but a framework of stainless steel tensioned cables can also provide support and enhance the aesthetic properties of the building. Site scented species over a door or train espaliered fruit along a wall and around windows. Whether a design is natural, formal, traditional or contemporary will determine the choice of plants and the method of training: informal vines can contrast with cut and sawn stone; a mass of honeysuckle can arch over a cottage; scented *Trachelospermum* can be formally

A slate wall at the Barnes Wetland in London creates a vertical transition between the mass of vegetation and the rough path. Numerous crevices provide shelter.

A whimsical fence and gate designed by Matthew Briton Grenyer, at the Thomas Shop, Penybont, mark the transition between one area and another, whilst keeping the continuity of the vegetation and allowing wildlife to move freely. ALISON GOULDSTONE

twined along cables up a rendered wall and *Pyracantha* trained into weird and wonderful shapes against brickwork.

At the base of a wall there is a transition that may be as rigid as brick meeting stone paving or as contrasting as stone meeting a verge of long grass, ferns, bare soil or garden planting of shrubs and herbaceous plants of differing heights. These transitions offer opportunities for the animals moving around to find the essentials of their lives – food, water and a mate.

Fences

The great variety of fences takes up much less space than hedges, which is an advantage in a small garden, but to benefit wildlife they need to be generously planted. Usually, fences are of solid wooden slats or boards that exclude plants encroaching from outside. More open trellis, palings or wires create possibilities for habitats to continue beyond the boundary into neighbouring spaces.

Plants that can cling to walls find it much more difficult to attach themselves to timber, so a network of wires is needed, which twiners can grip or be tied to. Espalier and cordon fruit work well against a fence and, while not evergreen, as they age, they develop a gnarled texture, as well as welcome flowers generous with pollen, nectar and fruit.

Recycling and Repurposing

Taking a sustainable approach to design and construction is increasingly important and is one of the first considerations when designing a garden for habitats. We discussed the 'as found' approach in Chapter 2 – starting with an evaluation of materials, trees, plants and habitats already on site and agreeing what can be retained or recycled. This approach can inform the choice of surfaces and structures in a garden and it is often possible to reuse materials in their existing form or repurposed as part of an innovative design, as we

Echinacea, loved by bees and butterflies, contrasts dramatically with a screen of reclaimed painted plywood.

In this Hebridean garden, gabions are used to create steps and a bench. All the rocks and stones were collected on site and reused.

In this design by James Fox, basalt strips are laid on a mix of soil and basalt chippings to create a contemporary path.
MARIANNE MAJERUS

Using recycled and repurposed materials			
Material	**Uses**	**Design attributes**	**Wildlife benefits**
Topsoil, sand and gravel	• Retain and spread on planting areas. • Add to new raised beds. • Use as a mix with other substrates to create mounds or to be laid between paving. • Use sand and gravel as substrates to create areas of the garden with different growing conditions.	Different levels, mounds, ridges and raised beds form masses and voids in the design. The use of soil with other substrates unifies areas of paving and gravel. In James Fox's design (pictured), basalt strips are set in a 40/60 mix of soil and basalt chippings to create a simple contemporary path that links with larger areas of paving.	• Possibilities for creating different soil structures and thus different habitats. • Opportunities for plants to seed between paving.
Crushed and broken paving, slate, roof tiles, ceramics, brick and concrete	• Use as a sub-base. • Re-lay as part of the hard landscaping. • In gabions to form retaining walls, steps and seating. • Crushed brick is light and porous so can be used in combination with other substrates on green roofs. • Vary the dimensions of the substrate to create areas with different growing conditions.	Large broken pieces of paving can be used to create an abstract crazy paving. Paving laid with porous gaps can form part of a SuDS-compliant front garden. Gabions can be used both formally and informally in rectilinear designs. Choosing similar materials to fill the gabions and create paths and paved areas helps to unify the space.	• Small cracks and crevices provide shelter. • Opportunities for plants to seed between paving. • Crushed concrete and limestone are lime-rich and low in nutrients, so are suitable for a wildflower scree garden.
Sand, gravel, clay	Rammed earth for: • Walls • Steps • Raised beds • Seating	Textures and colours layered through the walls add interest and can create links with other materials in the design. Using local materials creates a visual link with the wider landscape.	• Small cracks and crevices can be created to provide shelter. • Opportunities for plants to self-seed.
Hazel and willow – may not be available on site but can often be found locally	• Retaining walls • Arches and tunnels • Fences and trellis • Children's dens • Plant supports	Woven hazel and willow can be used to create vertical elements in informal designs. They combine sympathetically with a wide range of planting schemes.	• Small cracks and crevices provide shelter. • Using living and non-living willow and hazel provide different habitats and opportunities. • Twigs for nesting material.
Branches and tree trunks	• Fences and screens • Log piles • Steps • To fill gabions • Seating • Retaining walls • Play possibilities	Larger logs can be used to create low retaining walls in informal schemes and can be used in contemporary designs to fill gabions. Branches with distinctive shapes form vertical screening elements in the design.	• Small cracks and crevices provide shelter. • Rotting wood is a habitat for detritivores. • Provide habitats that support fungi, mosses and lichens.

(*Continued*)

(Continued)

Material	Uses	Design attributes	Wildlife benefits
Rocks and boulders	• In or near ponds • As a feature • To fill gabions • Steps • Informal seating • Retaining walls	The final placing of rocks is usually completed on site. They can be used to create contrasts with soft landscaping or to add to the reflections in a pond. Drystone walls can be designed to create organic shapes and sweeping curves.	• Small cracks and crevices in drystone walls provide shelter. • Larger rocks provide places for amphibians to shelter on edges of ponds. • Provide habitats that support mosses and lichens.

Rammed earth is used to form the walls is this dramatic design by Sarah Eberle for the Chelsea Flower Show 2007.

A textural mix of secondary raw-materials is used to retain the vegetated mounds, to create benches and as paths in this abstract design for Bridgefoot Street Park by Dermot Foley. PAUL TIERNEY

will demonstrate in the East London case study in Chapter 5.

The table (*above*) gives just a few examples of materials and the uses to which they can be put. Some secondary raw materials (*see* Bridgefoot Street Park case study later in this chapter) come under various legislative directives in the European Union and the United Kingdom and we do not have the space to discuss this here, save to point out that safety is paramount, and it is essential not to use anything that might be contaminated with hazardous waste. This applies just as much to the safety of wildlife as to humans.

Using Secondary Raw Materials

Landscape architect Dermot Foley's design for Bridgefoot Street Park in Dublin uses recycled materials to their full potential. Construction and demolition waste – secondary raw-materials – is incorporated in a variety of ways throughout the park. Waste material was sourced from depots across the city and seconds from the brick manufacturing process were also crushed to create substrates.

Open spaces, paths, steps, retaining walls, mounds and planting areas all benefit from his radical approach. He even uses bigger pieces of concrete as boulders. A key element of his design is its ability to exploit change. Foley explains, 'We simply do not know the exact characteristics of the secondary raw materials that will be brought on site' (2021: p.212).

Large, flat pieces can be used as surfaces or steps, creating a contemporary version of crazy paving. When designing habitats in gardens, these can be left with a smaller substrate in the gaps to be colonized by vegetation or become part of the planting design.

At Bridgefoot Street, some surfaces are formed of material with a smaller particle size – beneficial to seed germination. Foley (2021) also suggests spreading a layer of organic matter over recycled substrate to create areas for different types of plant communities. He points out that the pH and the moisture-retention ability also affect the habitats that develop on the site. Crushed concrete, for example, will not hold moisture, whereas brick is porous and traps water and air between particles (Emorsgate Seeds, n.d.-b).

We interviewed Foley and discussed the creation of the park during the latter stages of the build in the summer of 2021. He has specified larch and goat willow for use on the hills and described how he 'was inspired by how commercial forestry has been colonized at the edges by goat willow in certain parts of the west of Ireland . . . . I like the idea of using sort of brute commercial forestry species with wild, sometimes more delicate trees'. Larch was used for seating in the park, creating a subtle link between tree and timber.

Foley's creative incorporation of this broken and crushed waste demonstrates to designers the multiple ways in which hard landscaping materials may be recycled in gardens.

Design Tips

- Turn limitations into opportunities.
- Create hard landscaping habitat layers with surfaces, walls, pergolas and screens, and make the most of boundaries.
- Emphasize level changes.
- Reuse materials found on site or locally.

CHAPTER 5
***

SHELTER

Shelter is necessary for everything in the natural world to function. All animals need food, but they also are food and need hiding places and protection from the elements to have a fighting chance of getting to breeding maturity. Most animals, of whatever size, lead a life of forays into the exposed world followed by retreat into relative safety. In this chapter, we will look at how the designer can incorporate, within the layout and planting of the garden, those materials and locations that are needed for the animal occupants of the garden to nest, to burrow and to hide. Their need may be lifelong or temporary, or required for the time it takes for a stage of an animal's life cycle – for instance, pupation – to be completed. We will look at how the elements of shelter can be provided or enhanced by processes in the garden and by the types of planting that offer varied refuge.

Predators, weather and adverse temperatures all present dangers, but in remaining too sheltered, an animal risks starvation, dehydration or being cornered. Shelter and the other necessities of life, food and water, need to be found within an attainable orbit. For most insects and other small animals this is quite a small area; bees provide a notable exception, and honey bees may routinely travel a mile to reliable sources of nectar and pollen.

Many small birds have limited territory during their mating and parenting season, then make epic journeys in migration, some staying on the wing protected by speed and inaccessibility. Those that stop off on the way, for food and water, need to find cover in unfamiliar surroundings. In designing gardens to be hospitable to resident animals, and those passing through, a variety of resources needs to be available. The provision of shelter is one ingredient of the habitat of a particular animal or plant.

Habitats are to be found in every garden, intentionally or otherwise. In designing a garden, thought should be given to preserving such habitats that are desirable and integrating them with those newly created in a connected and harmonious way. In developing new habitats in the garden, we need to consider the baseline, which is comprised of microbes and detritivores, as well as the smallest animals and plants. At its simplest, this may involve growing grasses of different length, introducing hedges and allowing at least some of the waste and detritus from these to persist. In addition, a variety of heights, textures, spaces, crevices and cavities in the vegetation provide places to shelter. Moss, bark, leaves and grasses all provide materials for nest building.

To be effective, habitats need to be continuous or overlap, and this is as much a requirement of the

This sinuous dry hedge winds through woodland, making a corridor of shelter for hedgehogs and other small animals, and supporting detrivores as it rots into the ground.

design of a garden as is the provision of the materials and locations that offer shelter. By integrating the edges of vegetation types – close ground cover into low shrubs, or grasses into layered shrubs – the designer can create links, which we discuss later in this chapter. The winter landscape, with vegetation alive and dead, offers protection from temperature extremes, rain and wind. This is most valuable when there is continuity of vegetation in hedges and trees, and vertical and horizontal layers.

Overwintering

In Chapter 3, we discussed research conducted by the RHS on the relative value of different sorts of plantings to invertebrates in the garden. The *RHS Plants for Bugs – Bulletin 3* (Bostock and Salisbury, 2019) and Salisbury *et al.* (2020) summarized results from trial plots in relation to the invertebrate populations. Their findings show that effective planting for most ground-active invertebrates is dense with a mixture of native, northern hemisphere and some southern hemisphere plants, including some evergreens close to the ground. Ground-hugging *Cotoneaster dammeri* 'Oakwood', *Heuchera* and several evergreen *Euonymus* are useful in this respect.

The sort of shelter needed in winter may be quite different from that required in the warmer months. It needs to be sustained and durable and may be *in situ* or found as materials that animals can harvest. For certain animals it is key that their shelter persists for several years.

Animals have various strategies for maintaining their population through the winter. Insects, spiders, reptiles, worms, amphibians and many other small creatures that overwinter in our gardens are cold-blooded and slow down as the temperature drops. Their inactivity makes them vulnerable to predation by birds, battering by wind and rain, and freezing. Social bees can maintain a temperature such that they can remain active and venture out when there is enough warmth in the air. Bumble bees are usually the first to be seen visiting early flowers.

Various insects, such as aphids, overwinter as eggs. Many butterflies spend the winter as larvae or pupae, while red admirals and tortoiseshells, wintering as adults, do not become fully dormant and can wake up on warm days. It is vital for animals wintering as eggs to be able to eat as soon as they hatch, so the most successful parents lay the eggs close to, or on, food plants. Dense vegetation, dead or alive, facilitates this and is enhanced when spent stems and foliage are left either standing or on the ground. Seed heads and leaves, persisting as late as possible into the spring, offer food, as well as nesting places and safe havens.

The foliage of *Panicum virgatum* 'Rehbraun' lit up by low sun persists into the winter, sheltering small animals.

Many butterflies and other invertebrates need long grass during pupation, which may last over the winter, before emerging as adults.

Grasses, standing late into the winter, provide visual interest and presence in the garden at a time when the sun is low in the sky and highlights their warm and varied hues. *Calamagrostis × acutifolia* 'Stricta', *Molinia* 'Poul Petersen' and *Pennisetum alopecuroides* all maintain winter presence and are best placed where the low sun will catch their seed heads against a dark or uncluttered background – some evergreen planting or a hedge.

Ladybirds and other small insects overwinter as adults hidden in crevices – under tree bark, in hollow stems and in small gaps in stone and wood, even in window frames. They are amongst the many creatures that have adapted to profit from human activity and the measures we take for our own shelter. Soil is a home for many ants that delve below the frost line, insulated from sharp changes of temperature. Lawns provide the right conditions for this, but long grass is even more attractive to them.

Small mammals, such as dormice and hedgehogs, being warm-blooded, are stimulated to prepare for a period of hibernation when the temperature drops in the autumn. They eat to build up stores of fat and seek out protected locations to make nests or to take advantage of compost heaps and dried leaves.

Amphibians, being cold-blooded (ectothermic), can only maintain a temperature that is supported by external factors – the ambient temperature, the warmth of the sun. In the winter, they go to ground and may be found in compost heaps, under leaves or beneath anything else lying on the ground that offers a damp refuge, as it is important that they do not risk drying out. A few frogs and newts may stay in ponds over winter, risking freezing but being the first in line for mating when the females wake up.

Cold-blooded lizards, including slow worms, retreat to safe places where they can cool right down but be protected from freezing. They spend the winter in torpor known as brumation, in which they go through cycles of sleep and wakefulness. Soft places like compost heaps and leaf litter suit slow worms, while lizards favour places such as drystone walls from which they can emerge to bask when they feel the warmth of the sun.

Longevity

When designing gardens, it is important to bear in mind the length of time needed for habitats to develop in order for creatures to thrive. Where possible, try to retain existing habitats on site. The permanent or long-lasting elements of garden planting are the ones that give structure to the garden – the 'bones' that become more distinct in the hungry months. At this time of year, evergreens at every level shelter animals and create windbreaks that ameliorate the chill factor.

Death and Decay

The eggs of stag beetles are laid in rotting wood, where they hatch and live as larvae for several years, eventually pupating in the soil and emerging the following summer as adults. This is an example of an animal that is very specific in its needs. While we may make log piles in the garden, these can only help stag beetles if the logs are left to rot over the period of years that the larvae take to mature. Many other beetles, such as the useful slug-eating, violet ground beetle, follow a similar life pattern, spending the winter as adults in ground-plant detritus, leaf piles and at the base of grass tussocks.

Millipedes, beetles and other detritivores, the housekeepers of the food chain, are preyed on by all and sundry, and they keep the cycle of nutrients flowing from the dead and rotting vegetation they devour. In contrast, centipedes are nocturnal predators that prey on a wide range of small creatures, including spiders and slugs. At the same time, bacteria and fungi derive their nutrients from the detritus of plants and animals, dead or alive.

At all times of the year, moving stones or logs on the ground will probably reveal animals hoping not to be discovered, so the less disturbance the better for their chances of survival. Newts, frogs and toads, which spend only a short part of the year in water, are frequently found in these places, along with beetles, millipedes, centipedes and slugs.

While the ground layer is inevitably damp, some invertebrates seek out drier refuges. The remains of herbaceous vegetation left standing to decay are aerated and dry quickly – the hollow stems of fennel and other umbellifers, and many grasses, as well as the

A fallen trunk rots providing a substrate for moss and root runs for various small plants. Hollows under the bark harbour insects, fungi and detrivores. This is a long-lasting habitat for creatures such as stag beetles. MARIANNE MAJERUS

dried flower heads of shrubs such as hydrangeas, are long-lasting when allowed to persist. Like so many resources in the garden, density and mass is particularly valuable in winter and, used thoughtfully, are just as pleasing to gardeners as to animals.

Trees

The presence of trees is valued by human and animal inhabitants alike. Their form is a powerful driver of the visual setting and, as the dominant type of vegetation, their effect on the habitat is manifested in many ways. The shelter that trees afford comes from their textures, shapes, crannies, wounds and holes, as well as the leaf canopy and the leaves and twigs that fall to the ground.

To maintain a species population, every animal needs to reproduce sufficiently to ensure that at least two offspring from a breeding pair reach maturity. Aphids, which breed in an exposed and prolific way, allow for huge wastage, while birds, which produce their eggs in single figures, put great effort into providing and protecting a safe nest for their young. At this stage, shelter is of paramount importance to them. Most native British trees are deciduous, and their first flush of leaves in spring gives nesting birds cover. Native evergreen trees, such as box, holly and yew, harbour many hiding places for birds, but there is a relative paucity of evergreen natives in Britain. Non-native trees provide some of the densest cover. *Pittosporum, Cotoneaster, Laurus nobilis, Prunus laurocerasus* and *Arbutus* all conceal roosting and nesting birds, as well as providing flowers, seed and fruit. Their contrasting textures may be design features in themselves.

Each of these trees is distinctively shaped when allowed to grow naturally, but some may suit the designer's purpose better when pruned or clipped, which also has the effect of creating dense foliage and twigs. *Arbutus* is best left to create its multi-stemmed, domed shape unpruned.

Conifers, which encompass trees with a wide range of attributes, present dense and long-lasting cover for the garden, but must be selected with care. The very characterful *Chamaecyparis lawsoniana* 'Wisselli', with its distinctive crunchy texture and silver-grey needles, offers an appeal in complete contrast to the thuggish Leyland cypress (for which there is always a better

Elegantly contrasting treatments in a *Thuja* hedge at Anglesey Abbey create formality while linking with the woodland beyond.

alternative), but both are appreciated by roosting birds and insects that shelter in their bark. Scots pine and *Cupressus sempervirens*, best suited to the north and south of Britain, respectively, are distinctive in character and shape, and evoke quite different sensations in humans, and while we may appreciate the texture of Scots pine bark, its ruggedness also provides a home for crawling insects and other invertebrates.

Willow and birch are two of the earliest trees to break dormancy. Beech and oak are the latest but when kept as a hedge, retain their old season's leaves until the buds break in late spring – one of the many reasons that make a hedge a valuable habitat for wildlife. Conversely, when allowed to grow freely, box trees make dense and sculptural masses up to 12m high, offering thick, evergreen shelter to birds and other animals and pollen to bees.

At the time of writing, box has fallen victim to box caterpillar, originating in the Caucasus but delivered to Britain in plants imported from Europe. Designers must meet the challenge of finding substitutes for the large population of clipped box in gardens. *Euonymus japonicus* 'Microphyllus', *Teucrium* × *lucidrys* and *Sarcococca* ssp. are all candidates that offer a comparable and varied palette of design and wildlife attributes. A low-growing cultivar of the native yew, *Taxus baccata* 'Repandens', is also a possibility and some of the *Pittosporum* varieties, such as 'Golf Ball', lend themselves to hard pruning.

The bark of trees may be used as a distinctive design feature, most appreciated in winter, and

The shaggy texture of river birch bark provides tiny nooks for overwintering insects and nesting materials for birds.

particularly strong when repeated. Oak, crack willow, ash and elder, all have bark that is deeply fissured, while the peeling bark of birch offers softer nesting places. Tree trunks represent a path from the base to the canopy of the garden layers, and their permanence allows other plants and fungi to establish on and within them. Mosses, liverworts and lichens are a source of nesting materials for birds and small mammals and *in situ* can be hosts to small invertebrates. The highly specialized marbled beauty moth lays her eggs on lichens in trees, which is food for the hatching larvae. In decline, trees begin to offer a different range of substrates over a period. Senescent and fallen branches and dead twigs succumb to parasitic and saprophytic fungi, eventually ending up as rotten wood, essential to beetles.

All trees flower, but those that do not rely on insects or other animals for pollination have no need to expend energy in producing nectar, scent, or conspicuous flowers. *Buxus* and yew are wind-pollinated trees whose value to insects is principally in their evergreen habit, craggy wood and longevity, with the arils of yew seeds providing food for birds.

Birds do not hibernate, but they may migrate. In Britain, we gain some winter visitors, such as brambling, waxwing, fieldfare and redwing, from Continental Europe, and thrush and blackbird numbers are boosted by European birds taking advantage of milder winters. Robins, which seem so permanent, tend to shift southwards for the winter, though not necessarily very far. All these birds need trees to roost in, seeking the most sheltered places to conserve body heat.

A garden of layered vegetation with evergreen cover, framed by a *Magnolia*.

Hedgerows

A native mixed hedgerow is a natural boundary to make where a garden backs on to farmland. While being more suited to rural locations than urban, and requiring space

that not all gardens can afford, it is worth remembering all the benefits it can bring. A hedgerow is arguably the most concentrated source of shelter and food for small animals and birds, and some combinations of its qualities should be possible in most gardens. The sequence of blossom from cherry plum in February to dogwood in June is invaluable for insects. The fruit and nuts that follow attract birds and small mammals, and the leaves of hedgerow plants are food for the larval stages of many butterflies. Hedgerows create windbreaks and shade externally, and microclimates and rotting wood in their tangled middle, and dry soil, leaves and detritus at their base. Visually, they present a background that is solid but ever-changing. They can be managed for height and close-pruned or allowed to grow more informally, though they will always need management. Some of their constituents can be spared from pruning to grow into trees, which may be necessary for screening or for framing views.

Venturing Out

Emerging from their winter refuge, animals are vulnerable as prey to predators depleted of their own fat

Dense cover and a camouflaged edge for animals venturing out in spring.

Woodland Edge

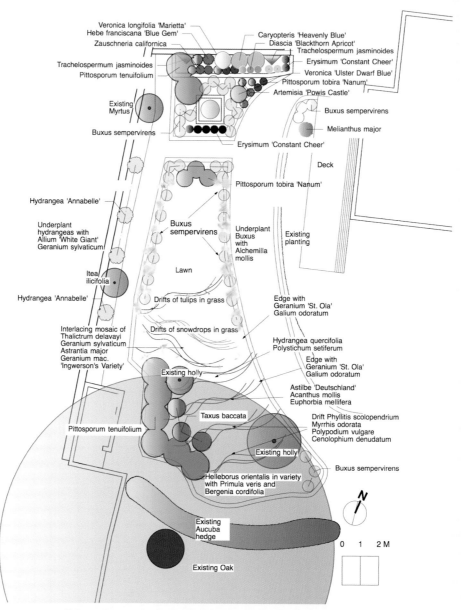

Veronica longifolia 'Marietta'
Hebe franciscana 'Blue Gem'
Zauschneria californica
Caryopteris 'Heavenly Blue'
Diascia 'Blackthorn Apricot'
Trachelospermum jasminoides
Trachelospermum jasminoides
Pittosporum tenuifolium
Erysimum 'Constant Cheer'
Veronica 'Ulster Dwarf Blue'
Pittosporum tobira 'Nanum'
Artemisia 'Powis Castle'
Existing Myrtus
Buxus sempervirens
Buxus sempervirens
Melianthus major
Erysimum 'Constant Cheer'
Deck
Hydrangea 'Annabelle'
Pittosporum tobira 'Nanum'
Underplant hydrangeas with Allium 'White Giant' Geranium sylvaticum
Buxus sempervirens
Underplant Buxus with Alchemilla mollis
Existing planting
Itea ilicifolia
Lawn
Hydrangea 'Annabelle'
Drifts of tulips in grass
Edge with Geranium 'St. Ola' Galium odoratum
Interlacing mosaic of Thalictrum delavayi Geranium sylvaticum Astrantia major Geranium mac. 'Ingwerson's Variety'
Drifts of snowdrops in grass
Hydrangea quercifolia Polystichum setiferum
Edge with Geranium 'St. Ola' Galium odoratum
Existing holly
Astilbe 'Deutschland' Acanthus mollis Euphorbia mellifera
Taxus baccata
Drift Phyllitis scolopendrium Myrrhis odorata Polypodium vulgare Cenolophium denudatum
Pittosporum tenuifolium
Existing holly
Buxus sempervirens
Helleborus orientalis in variety with Primula veris and Bergenia cordifolia
Existing Aucuba hedge

N

Existing Oak

0 1 2 M

This garden plan shows a graded planting from the shade beneath
the oak to full sun at the top of a south-facing slope.

(Continued)

(Continued)

Beneath the oak tree and close to its trunk we find plants such as *Aucuba*, which tolerate low light levels and root competition. Further from the trunk, but still well within the canopy, holly, *Skimmia* and yew thrive – evergreens that profit from the early spring when the oak is leafless. Hellebores and many ferns find the conditions beneath the edge of the canopy suit them, being both damp and, on the north side of the tree, in dappled shade. Beyond these, we find sweet cicely and woodruff, which thrive where they do not have to compete with more vigorous plants. In the grass, bulbs were planted in the lawn, where they grow fast and flower ahead of the first flush of grass growth.

Among the plants that can bridge the transition from shade to light are *Alchemilla*, *Hydrangea quercifolia* and some hardy geraniums, which tolerate a wider range of light levels and are strong competitors. The early flowering plants provide nectar and pollen at a critical time for emerging insects, as well as cover all year round. At the north end of these borders, the transition is into full sun, in front of a brick wall, where conditions are hot and dry and favour pollen gatherers throughout the summer, and provide places for spiders and other invertebrates that seek a dusty refuge.

stores. Shelter is equally necessary through the warmer months, but it may be more transient. In the growing season, plants are developing daily and offering more cover. Temperature and insulation become less of a problem, whilst access to food and water increase in importance. The geographer, Jay Appleton (1996), devised his theory of prospect and refuge as it applied to humans, but it can equally be seen as a strategy for survival in other animals. Every animal profits from the opportunity to survey the surroundings while hidden, which has led to the evolution of camouflage and disruptive markings. Edges and changes between vegetation types offer possibilities for seeing without being seen.

Invertebrates such as spiders find clearer spaces more conducive to ranging over their environment. Ground-nesting bees and some wasps need to burrow into bare ground and banks, while availability of mud is important to some birds in nest building. These are the sort of habitats commonly found on some brownfield sites where there has been clearance, natural disturbance and agricultural activity (Buglife, n.d.-a). As we have seen in Chapter 4, these sorts of habitats can be replicated on a small scale as scree gardens and gravel paths with edges that merge with planting. Low-growing Mediterranean shrubs, such as *Cistus*, *Genista* and lavender, work well in these conditions. Gaps behind sheds and beneath fences are also places where bare soil and stone can be left exposed.

Designing Corridors, Edges and Layers

Within the design of gardens, shelter for small animals should be provided in an integrated way, combining design elements for attributes beyond their use to wildlife. Qualities of plants are valued by humans and animals alike, for different reasons – texture, structure, layers and durability, all contribute to the quality of the human environment, as well as having survival potential for wildlife. In thinking about corridors and layers for wildlife, we are making use of the planes and vertical elements of the garden. The visual effect of horizontal lines in design is calming, while verticals are enlivening and stimulating. These are devices the designer can use to induce sensations and reinforce the character of spaces.

Through the warmer months, shelter needs to be flexible and varied, allowing animals to move about in relative safety. When trees and shrubs become clothed in leaves, the connections between the layers become more fluid. Plants such as *Cornus controversa* have a very marked layered structure, giving them a distinctive character. At a smaller scale, *Viburnum plicatum* 'Mariesii' displays the same outline. The effect of these is visually striking and brings into sharp relief the softer layers seen in Japanese maples or see-through trees, like birch and

Hungry mullein moth caterpillar, wasp HQ, hidden mouse (OLI HOLMES), hungry hare, huddling ladybirds, intrepid February bumble bee.

Cercidiphyllum japonicum, meeting taller grasses and perennials. Where layers connect, three-dimensional travel is possible for flightless animals. Nevertheless, it is visually important to maintain periodic spaces between layers to ensure that the vegetation retains form and character. There is a moment in late summer when gardens may lose their form and vegetation becomes amorphous, if structural elements in the design are lacking.

In the field layer, there are grasses and perennials that conspicuously echo the layered nature of planting. Umbellifers display their flat, open heads of flowers, and they are also amongst the best plants to leave standing in the winter garden, as they persist into the winter as hollow stems and attractive seed heads.

At ground level, dense planting leaves little soil exposed and ensures relative safety from predators for ground-living animals. However, bare soil is useful to birds and reptiles for basking, and some birds and bees seek mud for nest building. Spiders favour open conditions and travel fast where the going is smooth.

Hedges modify the environment and provide cover, especially important to birds. The density of an evergreen cypress hedge, or the mixture of textures and cover in a mixed hedge, create nesting places, nesting materials and often food in the form of berries and seeds. The base of a hedge is usually lined with useful detritus and soft materials. Dormice, hedgehogs and birds all appreciate these for their shelter and the prey that may be sheltering there. Hedges form a particularly useful form of linear connection and may form part of a corridor that reaches out into the wider landscape.

A particularly important transition is the one that animals must make to access water. Even the most formal pool can be home to marginal planting, which

In this woodland at Holbrook Garden, cover is dense and there is a succession of flowers and berries for food.

Striking birch trunks in spring amongst ground cover planting with some taller perennials designed by Kerry Guy.

The mowing line creates the strength of the design, and indicates the informality is deliberate and cared for.

East London Garden

This East London garden demonstrates how shelter can be provided within a small, contemporary space. The design expands on the objects and plants found there, intensifying the vegetation and the spaces.

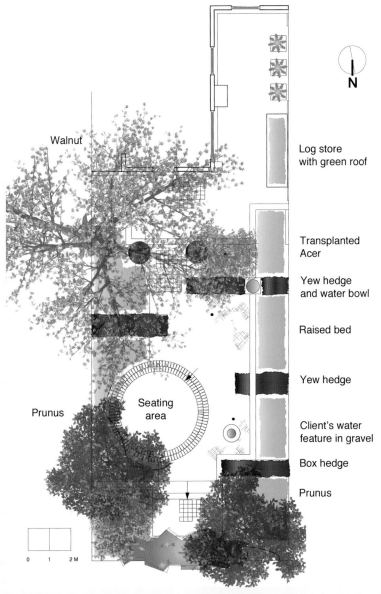

A plan for a woodland garden planting where cover is linked at all levels, water is provided and the views are framed with hedging.

(Continued)

(Continued)

The back of the garden is adjacent to a railway line, where verges and banks create a wildlife corridor and the borrowed landscape of mature trees. The existing garden trees include a large walnut, two *Prunus* and two transplanted Japanese maples, which provide a canopy and govern the light levels. The middle layers are then built up with yew hedging and shrubs – evergreens, such as box and *Mahonia*, with deciduous *Hydrangea quercifolia*, *Rosa rugosa*, lavenders and *Hebe*. These shrubs of different density and height provide a link to the tree canopies, while the ground-level planting provides shelter for invertebrates.

Ground cover of ferns, *Vinca minor*, *Alchemilla*, hellebores and dense, evergreen *Epimedium* maintain cover throughout the year and create a connection with, and between, the shrubs. Ivy on the boundaries is a constant dense presence linking with shrubs, ground cover and the existing trees. The steel screens set in grasses link visually to the seating and emphasize that the vegetation has been deliberately left tousled and impermeable to all but the smallest creatures.

A further layer is provided by the log store's green roof, planted with *Sedum*, *Luzula* and *Ajuga reptans* 'Atropurpurea'. In contrast to the dark damp places at the back of the logs, it is an environment like gravel, particularly attractive to spiders, being dry and relatively open.

Gabions retaining the raised beds provide a network of tiny, protected spaces between the gravel surface and the densely planted borders. The plants and soil in contact with the gabions create a further transitional environment, allowing movement under cover.

The design of the planting provides cover and food throughout the year for birds and invertebrates and, importantly, the vegetation is connected through the garden making corridors for crawling animals.

A bird bath where an *Acer* provides perches for waiting birds; the gabions create crannies for spiders, reptiles and insects.

A Cor-ten screen obscures the background; *Digitalis ferruginea* seed heads contrast in form and link through colour.

allows them to climb in and out. Informal pools, where gently sloping sides are integral to the design, still need marginal planting connected with land plants to maintain the cover. We will examine in detail the importance of access to water and its role in design in Chapter 7.

Woodland edges, pond edges, streams, hedge boundaries and walls are all examples of places where vegetation and materials change and transition into different habitats. These features serve the purpose of corridors, sheltering animals in motion, as well as at rest. The challenge for designers is in achieving joined-up habitats, when much of our pleasure in the garden is in having well-designed, open spaces.

Scaling the Layers

We have seen how maximum biodiversity is favoured by varied layers in vegetation. Not all insects have the flying capability of dragonflies. Some travel more easily on the wind and by raising themselves off the ground, may achieve a better lift off. The various species of ladybird are some of the many predatory beetles native to the UK. They may overwinter in the hollow of a broken cow parsley stem, rousing to launch themselves aloft on the breeze. They might alight on willow bark where they can feed on aphids and shelter there, where they may lay their eggs close to the aphid population, and eventually descend to the field layer of grasses and low herbaceous plants to prey on other small insects and their larvae.

In designing spaces for people, consideration is given to the ways horizontal layers affect our experience of ambience and space. The tree layer frames views, while the shrub layer encloses us; it is the field and tree layers that co-exist happily with circulation and use, and which we scan and walk over, or through. For animals, the layers are more fine-grained, needing connections to facilitate travel within their habitat. Flightless animals are mostly relegated to ground level, or below it, but they may climb walls, fences, stems and trunks to meet their needs for shelter and sustenance. Climbing plants create the means to do this under cover. Ivy is one of the best providers of dense foliage all year round, and nectar and pollen from its late flowers. As well as climbing over trees and fences, it may be used in a formal way.

In every garden, boundary materials form important vertical features and in a small garden they can contribute a large proportion of the useful surface area. As discussed in Chapter 4, the materials and design we choose for fences and walls are significant in the value they hold for wildlife.

The intersection between the qualities of plants appreciated by animals and those enjoyed by humans

A section drawing of the RSPB garden where furrows of mown grass and ridges of meadow grass create varied layers leading down to the wetland.

Precisely pruned ivy creates bold stripes and dense cover for insects and spiders.

Plants for shelter		
Plant name and origin	Wildlife value	Design attributes
Blechnum spicant Native	Adds to shelter amongst rocks.	Sculptural ground cover in shade.
Calamagrostis × *acutiflora* 'Karl Foerster' and 'Stricta' Non-native	Tussock-forming base has been known to be used as a hedgehog nest.	Vertical presence for much of the year. Seed heads stand into the winter.
Chamaecyparis lawsoniana 'Wisselli' Non-native	Dense evergreen cover.	Distinctive texture and upright form.
Cornus sanguinea Native and cultivars such as 'Midwinter Fire'	Shelter and fruits for birds. Berries high in antioxidants.	In a mixed hedge. Bright-coloured stems in winter.

(Continued)

(Continued)

Plant name and origin	Wildlife value	Design attributes
Cupressus sempervirens Non-native	Rough bark for sheltering insects.	Distinctive evergreen form in sheltered locations.
Deschampsia caespitosa 'Goldschleier' Cultivar of native	Good for nesting materials and shelter through the autumn.	Filmy texture adding to semi-transparent layers.
Epimedium perralchicum 'Frohnleiten' Non-native	Early nectar and pollen for bees, all-year-round shelter.	Evergreen ground cover for dry, shady places; yellow flowers in spring.
Euphorbia characias Non-native	Evergreen shelter. Likely to expand range with changes to climate.	Sculptural form throughout the year. Interesting colours.
Hippophae rhamnoides Native	Dense twigs for shelter and berries for wintering thrushes.	Good for structure and as a windbreak. Silvery leaves that contrast with bright orange berries.
Luzula sylvatica Native *Luzula nivea* Non-native	Dense rush for pollen and cover. Nesting material for golden eagles!	Airy rush for shade and damp places, semi-evergreen. *Luzula nivea* has attractive white flowers.
Myrtus communis Non-native	Attracts hoverflies; evergreen shelter.	Aromatic evergreen with attractive flowers. Sculptural trunk and attractive bark.
Pyracantha 'Cadrou' (formerly 'Saphyr Rouge') Non-native	Anecdotal evidence says birds prefer to eat red berries.	Mid-layer evergreen wall shrub with spring and autumn interest. Can be clipped to any shape.

is broad, and rather than limiting design, enhances it. Shelter that is useful to animals brings opportunities for design, in space, time and purpose, and an additional layer of thinking about the way design features interact. Just as continuity of shelter is important in habitats, harmony and highlights are valued in design. A long season of interest in the garden benefits all its inhabitants.

Design Tips

- Design using layers – consider the horizontal and vertical.
- Incorporate places where disturbance through tidying up is not necessary.
- Use a mix of native and non-native plants to ensure there is shelter throughout the year.
- Consider how longevity can be incorporated, for example, choose perennials and grasses with long-lasting seed heads.

CHAPTER 6

FOOD

Creating habitats in gardens to provide food for wildlife can be problematic. Attracting birds, bees and butterflies is recognized as worthwhile, but there are insects and invertebrates that feed on garden plants and are considered pests by many gardeners. It is worth remembering that some are themselves food: slugs and snails, aphids, caterpillars, midges and mosquitoes are all eaten by wildlife that we enjoy seeing in our gardens. We do not need to go out of our way to attract these invertebrates. But we can, and should, avoid using pesticides. We will discuss alternatives, such as biological controls, in Chapter 10. Providing habitats that are beneficial for the more charismatic creatures that eat the slugs and aphids can help to minimize the destruction of our favourite plants. Just one example demonstrates the importance of some of the wildlife that gardeners might try to exclude: one brood of blue tit chicks eats approximately 15,000 caterpillars (Butterfly Conservation, n.d.-d).

Birds, Berries and Seeds

When designing habitats for birds, we also need to create habitats that support insects, caterpillars, earthworms and other invertebrates. Birds can be thought of as natural pest controllers. At different times of the

year, they rely on a range of food sources. Foraging for insects and other invertebrates is easier in the warmer months but when the ground is frozen, this becomes more difficult. Some birds move to slightly warmer areas when they sense a cold snap is on the way. Changing location is not the only strategy, they also change their behaviour, flocking together, feeding faster and making the most of the daylight hours; it is essential that they build up fat reserves to get through the colder days and the periods of inactivity at night.

Female blackcap feeding on an *Amelanchier* berry.

Layers

As we have shown in previous chapters, an understanding of the importance of layers is fundamental to design. Trees support insects and provide fruits and seeds. When the ground is frozen, winter visitors such as redwings and fieldfares feed on berries in the canopy or on hips and haws in mixed hedges. Evergreens can protect the soil beneath from being covered in snow and thus make it more accessible for ground-feeding birds. The berries of trees and shrubs add colour to the garden in autumn and winter, and the insects and caterpillars living in their leaves are also food for birds. Species of *Berberis* produce long-lasting berries loved by thrushes and blackbirds, and finches enjoy the fruits of dogwood (Gardeners' World, 2019). Blackcaps are visiting gardens more often and pick the lower growing *Cotoneaster* berries. Climbers also support insects and some have berries and seeds. Black ivy berries last throughout the winter and honeysuckle produces red fruits in late summer. Antioxidants, found in many berries, help birds to sustain a physically active life and are an essential element of their diet (Gardeners' World, 2019). Rose hips especially, with their high levels of vitamin C, are excellent antioxidants, but they need to be left on the plant until they are ripe and squishy rather than being pruned out.

Dense layers of trees and shrubs support butterfly and moth caterpillars – an important food source for baby birds. As previously mentioned, blue tits consume huge numbers of caterpillars throughout the nesting period and time their breeding season to coincide with the peak caterpillar crop. However, the changing climate is affecting this delicate balance between leaf growth, caterpillar emergence and nesting birds (Springwatch, 2021); there is a phenological mismatch. If the spring is warmer, oak trees come into leaf earlier and caterpillars also respond to this increase in warmth. But blue tits (and great tits and pied flycatchers) are not able to lay their eggs in time to benefit, and nests can fail due to lack of food (Woodland Trust, 2018). It is interesting to note that baby blue tits also need more nutrient-rich spiders as part of their balanced diet (BBC Radio 4, 2021) – yet another reason to include a diverse range of habitats in the garden.

The field and ground layers are also important food sources for birds. Perennials and grasses attract invertebrates and seed heads provide winter sustenance. Many birds, including song thrush and blackbird, are ground feeders, and a flowering lawn is an invaluable habitat providing not only small seeds – grasses, plantain, buttercup and dandelion – but also a space for birds to poke around in the soil for earthworms and larvae such as leatherjackets. Jays hoard their winter food stocks in lawns and it is a habitat that is especially important for starlings.

Suffolk Woodland Garden

As we discussed in Chapter 2, this public garden was designed for the RSPB to demonstrate how wildlife habitats can be created in domestic gardens. The woodland area makes use of the existing mature birch tree and creates links with the alders, willows and poplars edging the river that flows below the garden. A curving hornbeam hedge protects the woodland habitat from the busy open area at the entrance to the garden where visitors congregate. This hedge encircles a small, secluded space under the birch, planted with ground cover and nectar-producing flowers. There are benches here so visitors can sit quietly and enjoy the colours, scents and wildlife. A water bowl provides a drink for thirsty birds and a semi-circle of posts with habitat niches has been designed among the planting; the little holes and crevices give shelter for insects.

Visitors follow the winding pine-needle path and are surrounded by woodland trees and shrubs. At their feet dots of colour carpet the ground and glimpses of the river appear through the trees. The plants provide shelter and are chosen for their fruits, seeds and berries. The mature tree layer is already in existence and this is enhanced with a *Sorbus aria* 'Majestica' and a *Populus tremula*. Tall, native shrubs, such as *Euonymus europaeus*, *Corylus avellana*, *Ilex aquifolium* and *Viburnum opulus*, bridge the mid and upper layers and provide berries and nuts. The decorative northern hemisphere plants, *Amelanchier lamarckii*, *Berberis wilsoniae* and *Cotoneaster lacteus*, also contribute to the supply of nectar and berries.

(Continued)

(Continued)

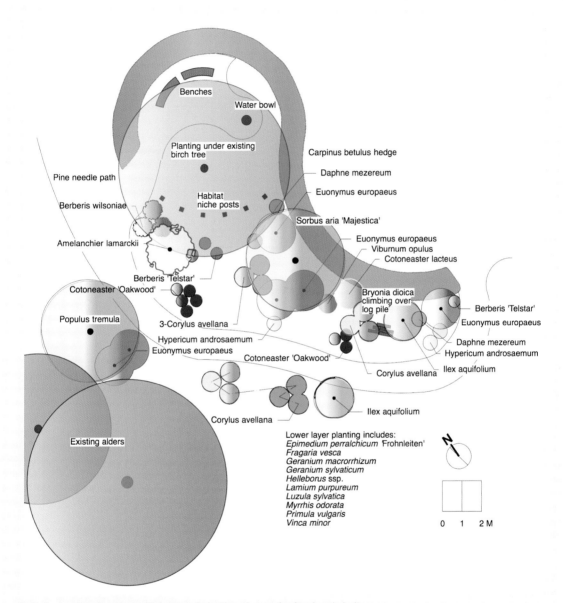

Benches
Water bowl
Planting under existing birch tree
Carpinus betulus hedge
Daphne mezereum
Euonymus europaeus
Pine needle path
Habitat niche posts
Berberis wilsoniae
Sorbus aria 'Majestica'
Euonymus europaeus
Viburnum opulus
Cotoneaster lacteus
Amelanchier lamarckii
Berberis 'Telstar'
Cotoneaster 'Oakwood'
Bryonia dioica climbing over log pile
Populus tremula
Berberis 'Telstar'
Euonymus europaeus
3-Corylus avellana
Hypericum androsaemum
Euonymus europaeus
Daphne mezereum
Hypericum androsaemum
Cotoneaster 'Oakwood'
Ilex aquifolium
Corylus avellana
Ilex aquifolium
Corylus avellana

Lower layer planting includes:
Epimedium perralchicum 'Frohnleiten'
Fragaria vesca
Geranium macrorrhizum
Geranium sylvaticum
Helleborus ssp.
Lamium purpureum
Luzula sylvatica
Myrrhis odorata
Primula vulgaris
Vinca minor

Existing alders

N

0   1   2 M

Suffolk woodland garden with layers of planting chosen for food and shelter.

There are fruits in the field layer provided by native *Hypericum*, bilberry, bearberry, *Daphne*, wild strawberry and non-native *Cotoneaster*. These mingle amongst a shade-loving, nectar-rich, ground-cover layer, of particular value in early spring. Once the tree canopy is clothed in new leaves, the light reaching the ground layer is reduced and growth slows. Dead nettles, wood cranesbill, sweet cicely and many other woodland herbs surge in growth and flower while light levels persist. At the bottom of the hornbeam hedge there are early flowering primroses and cowslips, and red valerian on the sunny entrance side.

(Continued)

(*Continued*)

View through fruiting *Euonymus* and hazel to the habitat niche posts.

As we discussed in Chapter 5, it is important to include some less closely tended habitats as places for invertebrates and mammals, such as hedgehogs and mice, to find food and shelter; rotting wood and vegetation, dying leaves and compost heaps all support invertebrates and in turn provide food for birds. In the Suffolk garden, hidden between the hazel and the holly, is a woodpile with white bryony scrambling through it, and fallen leaves are left on the woodland floor through the winter.

Decaying logs from the site are left amongst vegetation.

Marbled white on knapweed (SERGIO DENCHE), rose chafer climbing *Cenolophium*, rose chafer among meadowsweet, white-tailed bumble bee and *Echium*, early bumble bee exploring *Nectaroscordum*, small blue on tansy.

Insects, Nectar and Pollen

The most important foods for many insects, particularly those that fly, are nectar and pollen. Not all flowering plants are pollinated by insects, but those that are, put considerable effort into attracting their pollinators. In addition, many have evolved specialized mechanisms for making their flowers accessible and attractive to particular insects, which enhances the chances of pollen being transported to the stigmas of flowers of the same species. The shape of the flowers, and their colour and scent, are the principal ways that they attract the insects most useful to the purpose. Fortunately for us, these qualities are among those that humans most value in plants.

This close relationship between animals and plants is no accident. Flowering plants and insects evolved co-dependently; one could even say that each drove the increasing complexity of the other. For most insects, it is nectar that they seek, needing the sugar for energy throughout their active period, and the pollen that sticks to their legs and bodies is incidental. Bees, however, also actively seek protein-packed pollen to feed the larvae back home.

There are many lists of pollinator-friendly plants and yet there is little detailed research into the attractiveness of non-native plants or cultivars. This often leads ecologists and organizations to suggest that you should only plant native species. This is not necessarily the case; however, there are some basic rules to follow when designing habitats for pollinators:

- Create diversity with a wide variety of pollen- and nectar-rich flowers, including natives and non-natives.
- Include many different flower shapes – bees and other insects have tongues of different lengths.
- Ensure a wide range of flowering periods, even through the winter – bees can emerge as early as February and some are still flying in November.
- Avoid plants with double or multi-petal flower heads – the nectar is inaccessible and scent usually absent.
- Remember that healthy plants attract more insects – choose the right plant for the right place.
- Avoid the use of pesticides.
- Allow lawns to grow longer and retain lawn 'weeds'.

Bees

As we discussed in Chapter 3, Rosi Rollings' (2019) research is a useful starting point when deciding which plants to introduce for solitary, honey and bumble bees, and we have included some of her suggestions in our tables of suitable plants. Rosi points out that sterile plants, such as *Erysimum* 'Bowles Mauve' and *Helenium* 'Sahin's Early Flowerer', can also be a useful source of nectar. They have no pollen, but they continue to produce flowers and nectar, often for long periods. Although more research is needed, she notes that honey bees can dominate an attractive nectar source, out-competing other bees. A research project in the Netherlands also suggests that with the rise in urban beekeeping, there is a danger that honey bees are competing with native wild bees for scarce food resources (Pinto-Rodrigues, 2021).

Nectar is just sugar dissolved in water, and it might be expected that the sweeter the nectar, the more energy it contains and, therefore, the better it is. However, research has shown that for bumble bees this is not necessarily the case (Pattrick *et al.*, 2020). These bees drink the nectar and then vomit it up in the nest for others. Sweeter nectar is stickier and becomes more difficult to drink and very hard to offload back in the colony; the benefit of the high sugar content is outweighed by the energy expended by the bee.

Any analysis of nectar steps into the realm of scientific research; there have even been experiments to explore the possible impact of climate change on nectar secretion (Takkis *et al.*, 2015). The most important point for the designer to remember is to include a range of flower species and to include those particularly adapted to solitary bees and bumble bees. Rollings and Goulson's (2019) research also found that different bumble bee species preferred different plant cultivars. This could not be explained by tongue length alone and highlights the fact that there is still much we do not understand about the relationship between plant and pollinator.

Hoverflies

Hoverflies are also important pollinators. There are around 250 different species in Britain and some of

Shape

The different flower shapes and similar colours of *Phlomis russeliana* and *Digitalis lutea* contrast with the backdrop of yew in this design by Tom Stuart-Smith.

The variety of flower shape is visually stimulating to us and is an important component of the design of a border. By clustering flowers in a single head, as in the umbellifers and the mint family, or by fusing their petals into long tubes, like honeysuckle, flowers limit the range of insects for which they are useful. Even weight plays a part. While most flowers have a landing strip on which insects can alight, some like *Gaura* are flimsy enough to deter a heavy bumble bee; bees need to land on flowers to thoroughly clamber in and around them, as they do in snapdragons where the weight of certain long-tongued bees opens the flower, which then allows it to enter and be brushed with pollen, while getting at the nectar. Butterflies, with their delicate bodies, alight and use long probosci to access nectar from flattish heads of flowers like sedums, and some moths just hover, like hummingbirds in warmer climates.

Flowers with an open or flattish shape – umbellifers, *Achillea* and all the daisies in the *Asteraceae* family – are convenient to the light-weights of the insect world, in contrast to the sturdy *Digitalis*, *Eryngium* and *Eupatorium*, statuesque backbones to the border. While shape of the flower heads is critically important to their availability to particular insects, they also lend special character to a flowering border, from the calming effect of flat heads, the formality of round ones such as alliums, the fragility of grasses, the innocence of daisy heads, to the dominance of upright spires and plumes, like *Verbascum* and goldenrod.

their larvae are voracious predators of aphids. The adult hoverfly has simple mouthparts and no tongue, so feeds on flat, open flowers such as umbellifers. Fennel, *Astrantia*, *Selinum wallichianum* and varieties of aster are just a few examples of suitable perennials. In a design, umbellifers, with their wide, flat flower heads contrast well with vertical grasses such as *Molinia* 'Edith Dudszus' or with the purple globes of the tall *Allium* 'Purple Sensation'. Designers are not confined to perennials; apple and other fruit trees with large, open flowers introduce structure into the design whilst also attracting hoverflies and other pollinators.

Butterflies and Moths

Butterflies are generalists, taking nectar from a range of flowering plants – the greater the diversity of food sources, the more chance there is of attracting a variety of species. Try to create sheltered areas in the sun, as warmth is important, and select plants to ensure there are flowers throughout the seasons (Butterfly Conservation, n.d.-e). Butterflies need access to nectar as they emerge from hibernation in the spring, and autumn flowers will ensure they are able to prepare for winter. Deadheading prolongs the flowering season.

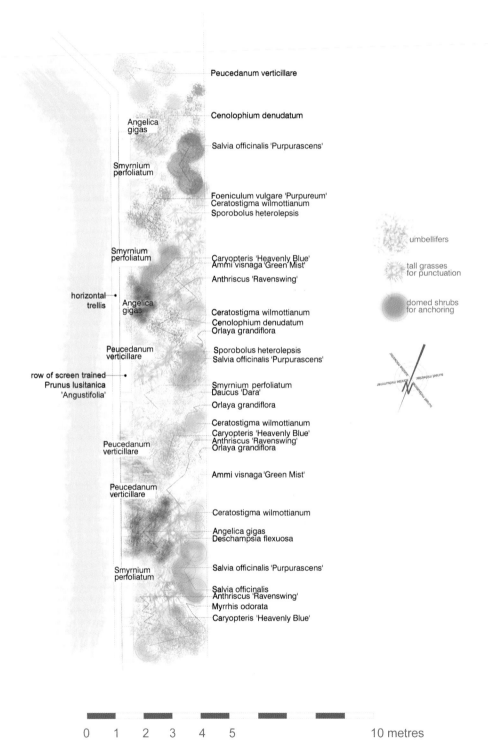

Peucedanum verticillare

Cenolophium denudatum

Salvia officinalis 'Purpurascens'

Angelica
gigas

Smyrnium
perfoliatum

Foeniculum vulgare 'Purpureum'
Ceratostigma wilmottianum
Sporobolus heterolepsis

umbellifers

tall grasses
for punctuation

Smyrnium
perfoliatum

Caryopteris 'Heavenly Blue'
Ammi visnaga 'Green Mist'

Anthriscus 'Ravenswing'

domed shrubs
for anchoring

horizontal
trellis

Angelica
gigas

Ceratostigma wilmottianum
Cenolophium denudatum
Orlaya grandiflora

Peucedanum
verticillare

Sporobolus heterolepsis
Salvia officinalis 'Purpurascens'

row of screen trained
Prunus lusitanica
'Angustifolia'

Smyrnium perfoliatum
Daucus 'Dara'

Orlaya grandiflora

Ceratostigma wilmottianum
Caryopteris 'Heavenly Blue'
Anthriscus 'Ravenswing'
Orlaya grandiflora

Peucedanum
verticillare

Ammi visnaga 'Green Mist'

Peucedanum
verticillare

Ceratostigma wilmottianum

Angelica gigas
Deschampsia flexuosa

Smyrnium
perfoliatum

Salvia officinalis 'Purpurascens'

Salvia officinalis
Anthriscus 'Ravenswing'
Myrrhis odorata
Caryopteris 'Heavenly Blue'

0   1   2   3   4   5   10 metres

This border of green, blue, white and mauve umbellifers, low-domed shrubs and dramatic grasses against an evergreen backdrop has been designed for pollinators.

Speckled wood butterfly feeding on *Sedum spectabile*.

Caterpillars are more specific in their requirements. It is this that has led to the belief that a wildlife garden must have a nettle patch. Red admiral, peacock, small tortoiseshell and comma caterpillars all feed on nettles. However, most gardens are too small to provide a large enough patch of nettles to create a suitable habitat (Gaston *et al.*, 2005). The caterpillars like to shelter in the centre of a patch and need to be in the sun (RSPB, n.d.). Food sources for other species are easier to introduce but before doing so, check that the adult butterfly is known to live in the local area. *Cardamine pratensis* can be planted at the edge of a pond or in a damp part of the garden to attract orange-tip and green-veined white butterflies. The common blue eats *Lotus corniculatus*, which can easily be introduced into a flowering lawn (Butterfly Conservation, n.d.-b). Leaving grasses to grow tall benefits the gatekeeper and meadow brown caterpillars. In the mid and upper shrub and tree layers, holly and ivy support the holly blue, and *Frangula alnus* is home for brimstone caterpillars (RSPB, n.d.).

Caterpillars are permanent residents in gardens, whereas butterflies and, to a lesser extent, moths are usually stopping off for nectar before moving on. They contribute to the ecosystem as pollinators, as food for birds and, especially at nesting time, bats and hedgehogs (Butterfly Conservation, n.d.-d). Although not all adult moths feed on nectar (some are so short-lived that they do not feed at all [Butterfly Conservation, n.d.-f]), those that do are attracted to some of the same plants as butterflies and also benefit from the nectar of night-scented species such as *Lonicera*

periclymenum, *Oenothera biennis* and *Hesperis matronalis* (Tonhasca, 2020). The length of the moth's tongue determines whether it can access the nectar. The highly decorative *Nicotiana sylvestris* has long, inaccessible, tubular flowers (only beneficial to the non-native convolvulus hawk moth), whereas the shorter flowered *Nicotiana alata*, although from the southern hemisphere, attracts native moths (Butterfly Conservation, n.d.-g). As with butterflies, moth caterpillars are specialists, feeding on particular leaves and grasses. Adult moths form an important part of the diet of bats, as do smaller night-flying insects (The Bat Conservation Trust, 2021), including the small flies that we may overlook, though many play a part in pollination as well.

Designing for Pollinators

The design of garden habitats for bees, butterflies, moths and other insects is not only about selecting the right plants. Where there is space, it is beneficial to plant in blocks or drifts so that there are many flowers at slightly different stages of development. We also pointed out in Chapter 3, Rollings' observation that bees prefer clusters of the same flower in order to maximize the amount of nectar they can access for the minimum effort. Perennials with a long flowering season may be more beneficial than those that have a short dramatic display, especially in a small garden.

For the designer, the shape and colour of flowers can be mixed and matched to create effects of visual

The strong vertical form of the fox tail lilies contrasts with the softer dynamic textures of *Stipa gigantea*.

delight. Pairing flowers of the same colour and different shapes, gives us combinations that are both subtle and attractive – *Geranium* 'Mrs Kendall Clark' and *Nepeta faassenii* have flowers of the same colour at the same time, which accentuates the contrast in their shapes. Orange flowers, and their subtle shades in the flattish *Achillea* 'Terracotta' and spires of *Eremurus* 'Cleopatra', highlight each other's shape, while fortuitously being attractive to a variety of different insects. Pairing attributes, in common and in contrast, is one of many useful devices for designers to draw on, and one that does not need to be restricted to flowers; it applies to all the many characteristics of plants.

Colour and Scent

The subject of insect vision and their perception of colour is fascinating and related to the way insects and flowering plants have evolved in tandem. Perception of colour in people is one of the great delights of gardening and one of the key components of the design of borders. The markings on petals give them distinctiveness and pleasure to the observant human, but there are further signals important to insects that are invisible to us.

The colours of the parts of flowers are determined by a complex mixture of chemicals, of which the most important in flowers are: the anthoxanthins, perceived by us as ivory white; anthocyanins, which we see as purple, red and blue; and xanthophyll and carotene, which are yellow and orange to us (Proctor and Yeo, 1973). The spectrum of light visible to insects is largely of a higher frequency, up to ultraviolet. The purpose of the markings on petals is to guide insects to nectaries, often hidden deep in the flower, accessible only to the long proboscis of insects such as butterflies and moths. Hoverflies are preferentially attracted to white and yellow flowers, bees favour violet and blue flowers, and, although thought to be oblivious to red, that does not stop them visiting red flowers, drawn perhaps by scent and shape. Scientists have also found that some flowers of different colours produce what they term a 'blue halo' around the centre of their petals that attracts bumble bees (University of Cambridge, 2017). This halo, invisible to humans, is formed when a series of ridges on the petals scatter the light, creating a blue/ultraviolet pattern – another way in which bees and flowers communicate.

A further strategy for selecting their favoured visitors is the fragrance that flowers emit. Scents are the result of a mixture of volatile oils produced within the flower, attracting insects from a greater distance than they can see, advertising the presence of nectaries (Proctor and Yeo, 1973). This seems to be a very specific trait, more finely tuned than humans can discern, and there may be scents that we cannot detect at all. Nevertheless, it is a further layer of delight to be considered in design, from the heady scent of honeysuckle and *Pittosporum* at night, timed for moths, and *Buddleia*, strongest at midday when butterflies are most active.

Plants cannot be considered garden worthy solely on the attributes of their flowers, but their flowers are certainly important to us. Flower colour, scent and shape are just three of the variables to consider when making plant choices, and the skill lies not only in selecting them, but in combining them to enhance their qualities by associating them beneficially and extending the season – benefiting insects, as well as ourselves.

A close-up of the bee guides and a solitary bee on *Geranium* 'Rozanne'.

Structure and Planting Layers

It is important to consider the structure of the planting areas and the ways they link together: the different layers from canopy, through the upper, mid and field layers to the ground, the diversity of planting and the maintenance. Structure can be introduced in the form of walls, vertical screens, obelisks and pergolas, all of which support climbing plants. *Lonicera* 'Belgica' and *Lonicera* 'Serotina', cultivars of the native honeysuckle, provide nectar with early and late flowers, respectively, and climbers such as clematis, honeysuckle, hop and ivy form the transitional layer and are also important food sources (Butterfly Conservation, n.d.-a). In the case of clematis especially, it is not only the native species that are hosts to caterpillars, cultivars are also suitable, although human visitors may not appreciate the nibbled leaves.

Mixed hedges of hawthorn, blackthorn, hazel, barberry, beech, spindle and privet are also excellent for a range of caterpillars (Butterfly Conservation, n.d.-c). In small spaces, design hedges that can be trimmed in places with contrasting sections left slightly unkempt. Leaving fallen leaves and twigs in parts of the garden provides shelter for caterpillars and pupae through the winter. Designing some areas of the garden to be less

Formal lines of clipped box frame the exuberant colours of low flowering shrubs and perennials, including *Achillea*, *Verbena*, *Echinacea* and *Perovskia*, all chosen for their attractiveness to pollinators.

Getting Up Close

The Walled Garden at Scampston in Yorkshire epitomizes the design philosophy of Piet Oudolf. He uses perennials and grasses with seed heads that remain standing through the winter months, providing shelter and food for wildlife and interest for human visitors. Designing with perennials with strong stems and long-lasting seed heads adds a dramatic aesthetic to a winter garden, especially when seen in low sunlight or coated with frost.

The dense planting at Scampston is designed to envelop and enclose a paved seating area with low chairs bringing the sitter up close to the flowers, the more easily to observe and enjoy the bees and butterflies. Plants are arranged in large groups of a single species and include *Amsonia tabernaemontana* var. *salicifolia*, *Panicum virgatum* 'Shenandoah', *Phlomis russeliana*, *Sedum* 'Matrona' and *Sesleria autumnalis*. The walled garden is divided with formal beech hedging, clipped to provide a contrasting backdrop for the perennials and also ensuring that there is plenty of cover, even in winter.

An enclosed seating area at Scampston in Yorkshire, designed by Piet Oudolf, brings the visitor into close contact with planting that encompasses the field and tall herbaceous layers.

manicured ensures that there are some taller grasses and wild flowers, such as bedstraws, dandelions and trefoils, that are attractive to caterpillars.

However, designs need not be informal; exuberant perennial schemes can be contained within low, clipped, evergreen shrubs and a formal herb bed in the sun is a good source of nectar. Many of the flowers, shrubs and trees that support pollinators are also attractive to humans. Designers can make the most of this by bringing people into close contact with the planting, so that they can enjoy the shapes, colour, scent and wildlife. Climbers can be trained around doors and windows, seating areas and paths can be surrounded by dense planting, structures for climbers form focal points and, in some cases, food for wildlife is also tasty for humans.

Flowering Lawns

We will discuss lawns and meadows in Chapter 8, but it is worth noting here the results of the Plantlife research,

A bumble bee collecting pollen and nectar from a plantain in grass that has been left unmown in front of these blocks of flats in London. SERGIO DENCHE

Every Flower Counts (Plantlife, 2019). Research participants in the United Kingdom counted the flowers in one-metre quadrants in their lawns across the UK. In all, 203 different species were recorded. The most common nectar-producers were: white clover, dandelion, red clover, daisy, selfheal, oxeye daisy, cat's-ear and hawk-bit. Most lawns (80 per cent of those surveyed) provided enough nectar to support an average of 400 bees. However, the remainder were found to support ten times this number – 4,000 bees. Plantlife's findings showed that:

- Only mowing with high blades every four weeks gives the highest nectar production – this benefits plants like white clover, daisy and selfheal.

- Leaving grass unmown resulted in a greater diversity of flowers and extended nectar availability – plants such as oxeye daisy, scabious and knapweed responded to this regime.

With minimal design interventions, the lawn can become a transitional space moving from a ground to a field layer and back again. At its simplest, mowing sections of lawn in rotation, and always keeping one area of longer grasses and flowers, is most beneficial.

Fruit Trees

In Chapter 9, we will discuss orchards, which few gardens can accommodate. However, one or more fruit

An ancient espaliered pear is trained along a flint wall at Wiveton Hall in Norfolk.

trees can hint at their evocative atmosphere, while contributing many benefits to wildlife and to us. Pollen and nectar are generously provided by the flowers of fruit trees, from *Prunus cerasifera* in February, blackthorn in the hedgerow in March, plum and pear blossom in early April, followed by apple blossom in May.

Most fruit can be trained and shaped, thanks to rootstocks that confer different degrees of vigour to the plant. Pruning of the young plants can then produce forms to suit every size of garden, lending structure to the ground plan, guiding the eye and

expressing the season. Nut trees, hazel and cob, can be coppiced or pollarded to make a strong shape or a small-scale avenue providing ample pollen as well as nuts.

Fruit trees can also be trained on wires or along walls – as fans, cordons or espaliers. As with the parasol trees, which we will discuss in Chapter 9, introducing fruit trees in this way creates an element of formality and makes the most of small spaces, whilst still contributing to the wildlife habitats of the garden.

Formally trained espaliers stand out against the orange wall in this garden designed by Arne Maynard.

A cultivar of the native hawthorn, *Crataegus laevigata* 'Crimson Cloud', attracts pollinators to its brightly coloured flowers. In autumn the haws provide food for birds.
BETH MINDEL-HOLMES

Plants for food		
Plant name and origin	**Wildlife value**	**Design attributes**
Abelia × *grandiflora* Non-native	Late-flowering food source.	Semi-evergreen structure with scented flowers.
Crataegus laevigata 'Crimson Cloud' Cultivar of native	Late spring flowers provide food. Berries high in antioxidants.	Useful tree for smaller gardens. Colourful flowers and haws.
Cynara cardunculus Non-native	Good food source for bumble bees and butterflies.	Sculptural silvery leaves and flowers. Dead seed heads remain through the winter.
Eryngium maritimum Native	Good food source for butterflies.	Architectural flowers and leaves. Dramatic colour.

(Continued)

(Continued)

Plant name and origin	Wildlife value	Design attributes
Erysimum 'Bowles Mauve' Non-native	Good food source for bumble bees and butterflies. Note that this is a sterile plant but is still a source of nectar.	Attractive, long-flowering perennial that looks good in groups with other purple and blue flowering plants and silver grey leaves.
Filipendula ulmaria Native	Food for larvae of several moths. Many insects attracted to flowers.	Frothy cream flowers combine well with *Lythrum* and other pink/purple flowers in interlacing schemes, especially at pond edges.
Geranium 'Rozanne' Cultivar	Food source for solitary bees and honey bees (top scorer in Rosi Rollings' research).	Fast-growing ground cover. Long flowering period. Can be used in formal and informal schemes.
Helleborus foetidus Native	Early flowers for emerging queen bees.	Sculptural leaves and unusual coloured flowers. Useful in shade. Self-seeds.
Origanum vulgare 'Aureum' Cultivar of native	Good food source for pollinators and butterflies.	Low-growing, bright yellow leaves and long flowering period. Good in combination with *Alchemilla* and *Nepeta*.
Phlomis russeliana Non-native	Good for bumble bees and provides winter shelter.	Vertical stems of yellow flowers create accents and unusual forms in winter.
Selinum wallichianum Non-native	Attracts hoverflies and other pollinators.	Tall, white flowers above feathery foliage. Contrasts well with clipped green shrubs.
Veronicastrum virginicum Non-native	Good food source for honey bees.	Strong, vertical form and long-lasting flower heads.

Design Tips

- Design spaces where people can get up close to experience the plants and the wildlife.
- Use non-native plants to extend the season – visually and with a supply of nectar.
- Think about different flower shapes for different types of insect.
- Leave areas of grass to grow longer.

CHAPTER 7

WATER

Not all animals drink, but every living creature needs water to metabolize. It may be taken from the air, sucked up as nectar or absorbed through their skin, but animals cannot do without it. Similarly, plants depend on water, which may be taken up by their roots or absorbed through the epidermis or cell walls. In this chapter, we will examine the many ways in which water is an attractive feature in the garden, an invitation to wildlife and a solution to problems that may arise as result of run-off. In many cases, we seek to tick all these boxes in a single water feature.

Ponds and Water Features

Water holds mystery and mood in its many states, valued by humans for regulation of air temperature, space and openness, sounds, reflections, excitement and tranquillity. Water offers entertainment and fun, as well as contemplative moments and aesthetic stimulation, and is incorporated into gardens in many ways.

To be useful to wildlife, water needs to be not just present, but accessible and of the right quality. Ideally, the condition of the water would be self-regulating, given the right balance of temperature, shade, aeration and nutrient levels. Advice on maintaining a healthy pond is beyond the scope of this book, but we can give some pointers.

A still pool with perfect reflections of the rocks. *Hosta* and ferns are placed to allow animals and birds to access the water.

A swallow hunting for insects over a still pond. ADAM CLARKE

Siting Pools and Ponds

Still water creates the best reflections, and siting it with reflections in mind and a place from which to observe them, rewards some attention to simple geometry. To bring light into a dark corner, water is the best surface, moving or still. It is the most peaceful surface to con-template – responding to a breeze, to the rising or dipping of insects and birds, with ripples indicating the activity of amphibians below the surface. Every child knows that water in a pond is teeming with life, but the design of ponds needs to reflect the ambitions we have for it at the outset.

In siting water, we need to recognize human and wildlife considerations and how we can combine them to best effect. We need to consider whether a pond is to look natural, sitting in a low point in the lie of the garden or at the base of a slope where water would collect naturally. Water at the top of a slope looks unconvincing unless it is starting a journey downwards to join a larger body of water. Formal ponds may be the key feature of the garden, sited to lead the design layout. Water features make compelling focal points, creating effects disproportionate to their volume. A brimming water level, where the water meets plants, paving or shingle on what appears to be level ground is beneficial to animals and creates the most pleasing visual and biological relationship between water and land. This is even more important in contemporary pools where there may be less camouflage of plants at the margins. A pool does not have to be informal to be

A small formal pond where rocks enable aquatic animals and larvae to hide and bask, and land animals to drink. MARIANNE MAJERUS

attractive to wildlife. Formal ones can be just as bene-ficial, as long as there are places where animals can creep in and out of the water safely, the water quality is suitable, and there is some shade and cover.

While shade is beneficial to maintain some cooler areas of water, the leaves from overhanging trees intro-duce excess nutrients. Water low in nutrients maintains clarity and is less likely to suffer from algal bloom. Shade may also be created with emergent and floating plants. Floating frogbit and deep-water arrowhead provide shade, while water-lily pads provide places for insects to alight in addition to cool dark depths.

Safety

Where there is open water, there is potential for acci-dents, but it is possible to design water features to be safe for children. While balustrades around, or grills

A natural pond surrounded by grasses and perennial plants. The mown paths give form to the slope, and a place for humans to get close to the water.

A bold stone path along the line of a rill, allowing continuity of wet places and running water in Le Jardin d'Agapanthe, Normandy, designed by Alexandre Thomas.

over, ponds may make them inaccessible, they are unlikely to enhance the intention of the water feature. Responsive design instead stimulates ideas for making water inaccessible more safely, while still allowing access and amusement. While the principal of 'walk in, walk out' with shallowly shelving edges may work for school-age children, there is no substitute for supervision of children near water.

A rill is a way of introducing water that cannot trap a child, while offering chances to play with it, to dam it and to race boats in it. To be available to wildlife, it is necessary to interrupt the flowing water with deeper reservoirs, which can be filled with rocks, making the water appear shallow, but allowing places for birds and amphibians to access it, providing deeper places where the water is shady and cool.

Raised pools allow open water, which is relatively safe for small children, and attractive to 'mess about' with, while adults appreciate the way water is brought close to eye level, particularly when seated nearby. Water lilies suit this sort of formal pool and give insects a place to alight. While it is possible to unobtrusively create means of getting in and out of the water, the outer edge presents problems for flightless animals. Planting shrubs and tall grasses

against the outer wall can provide the cover necessary.

In the smallest gardens, bird baths make a garden appealing to birds and can be sited where they can be watched from indoors. Keeping the bath full and the water clean is the only maintenance required for something that can give hours of interest. Bigger bowls attract more animals, but access and escape must be catered for.

Moving Water

The sound of moving water may be restful or stimulating, even dramatic, but a soothing trickle is what most people seek from a garden pond. Most formal arrangements of water in the garden have their origin

A robin enjoying a bath where densely planted layers allow birds to scan the surroundings for danger. Bird bath designed by Sarah Walton.

Woodland Waterfalls

This garden for Liseberg Amusement Park in Sweden was designed in collaboration with landscape architects, 02landskap. Liseberg is a popular amusement park with many attractions. However, a substantial part of the site was inaccessible to the public, covered with mature woodland growing on steep, rocky slopes. The brief was to create an exciting walk through the woodland that would draw people into different spaces, where they could relax in a more natural setting than that found in the rest of the park. It was essential that all the trees were retained, and that the soil and rock levels were not disturbed. This dictated the ways in which people moved around the space, the levels, steps and slopes.

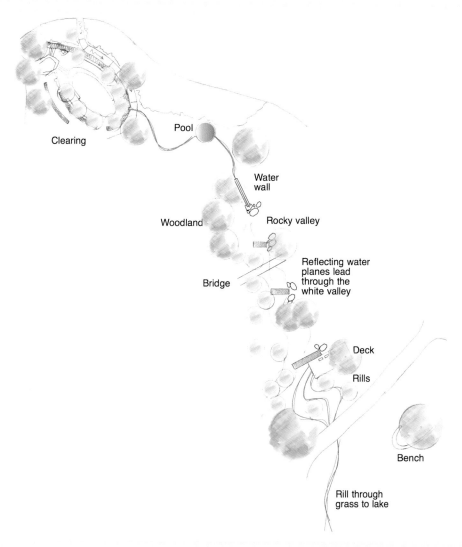

A plan for a water garden winding though rocks and natural gullies at Liseberg Amusement Park.

(Continued)

(Continued)

At the top of the site, an elliptical clearing has been created with new trees, walls and cantilevered seating. From here a path leads downhill, following and crossing the water. The design juxtaposes contemporary waterfalls with the existing trees and rocks. A stream flows along a high stone wall before falling into a rocky pool and disappearing. It re-emerges as shallow reflecting planes of water crossing smooth rectilinear blocks of stone and then falling again. This rhythm of reflection, falling and disappearance is repeated down the valley. Finally, three curving streams emerge, wind among the vegetation and join to form a single rill that flows through mown grass to a lake at the bottom of the site.

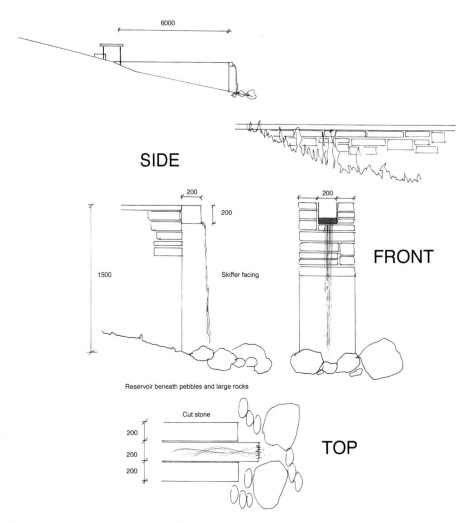

Elevations showing details of the water wall.

(Continued)

(*Continued*)

Materials link the contemporary elements of the garden with the existing landscape: the stone is local and laid with gaps that will be colonized by ferns and other small plants. The planting, much of it native, is chosen to replicate a woodland floor and white flowers bring light to these shady areas. The falling water, rocks, stones and pebbles create damp habitats for woodland creatures, as well as providing a respite for the public from the summer heat and the hard surfaces in the rest of the park. Although the park is often busy, keeping the mature trees and the large steep areas of rock and vegetation ensures that there are sheltered places for wildlife that remain relatively inaccessible to the public.

The water wall and bridge in a natural setting. Bridge design by 02landskap.

in natural phenomena. Natural springs seeping or bursting through the ground are echoed in water sources situated in a wall, trickling or spouting into a pool below. Fountains enliven the water and aerate it, but the splash created must be contained within the area of the water's surface. The volume of water in motion, the height of the head and the type of nozzle control this, but a limited flow, which leaves much of the pond undisturbed, is best suited to encouraging wildlife, if a fountain is part of the design. Water that trickles down a wall or other surface into water makes the least disturbance, while also aerating the pond.

Flora and Fauna

The Animals

Most garden wildlife is better adapted to still or gently flowing water and may only spend part of their life cycle in or on the water. Water in which microscopic animals, plants and detritus settle has the potential to support a myriad of insects, amphibians and birds, with the greatest diversity of creatures found in the shallows – water even just 100mm deep (Williams *et al.*, 2018). Deeper water, up to 600mm, supports larger invertebrates, and the underwater plant life, as well as

Frog (ELLIE MINDEL), mayfly (SERGIO DENCHE), mating damselflies, peacock butterfly and tadpoles, preening pigeon, newly emerged Southern Hawker dragonfly.

aerating the pond, provides habitats for water beetles and amphibians.

A diversity of animals requires a diversity of habitats, and rather than being one habitat, a pond is a mosaic of mini-habitats. In gardens, space for a pond may be restricted, and the draw-down area (the margin, where water levels may fluctuate) is often limited. It is useful to create a variety of depths with shelves in garden ponds. A bigger pond may be able to accommodate an island, resulting in more edge and variation in depth.

Many insects spend only their egg and larval stages in the water. Dragonflies, damselflies, pond skaters and many others emerge from the water for their last moult as flying adults. Frogs, toads and newts climb out of the water as young adults to live as terrestrial animals, returning to the water to mate. For all these animals, the edge of the pond is key. Some formal ponds may lack a sloping edge, so plants and stones should be positioned at places around the edge to enable creatures to climb in and out. As we have seen, the more shallow the water, the better for diversity. Shelves in the contours of the pond can be created using slates placed on bricks; they are unobtrusive, will support marginal and emergent plants, and create not only the effect of shallow water, but also a shady place beneath them. This serves as an additional habitat for animals that prefer cool, dark waters.

As well as the animals that need to live in the pond, there are those that need to visit it to eat and drink. Birds such as goldfinch, chaffinch and robin can be seen dipping into the water. Hedgehogs will come to the edge to drink, and some butterflies and moths need to take up salt by 'puddling' in shallow muddy water. It is interesting to note that aquatic insects have higher levels of beneficial unsaturated omega-3 fatty acids than terrestrial insects. Research undertaken over twenty-four years into the breeding success of swallows concluded that chicks fed on aquatic insects had a better chance of fledging (Twining *et al.*, 2018). As with humans, it is important to remember that food quality is as important as food quantity when providing habitats for wildlife.

The Pond Cycle

The best way to create a healthy pond is to ensure that there is an interconnected food chain between the plants and animals that it supports. At the base of the chain is organic detritus that supports crustaceans and insect larvae, and bacteria that live on the roots of marginal plants. Sunlight stimulates the growth of algae – which is food for water fleas, beetles and snails – as well as being absorbed by submerged plants that in turn oxygenate the water. The water flea is fundamental to the life cycle of invertebrates in the pond; it is food for creatures such as water beetles and pond skaters, which are eaten by dragonflies and aquatic amphibians. Dragonfly and damselfly larvae feed on invertebrates and may be eaten by fish and frogs. Tadpoles are also eaten by fish and make a snack for garden birds visiting the pond. In urban gardens, sparrows swoop down to catch damselflies on the wing and in larger ponds, swallows benefit from the insect life. Frogs catch insects and slugs in the surrounding undergrowth and herons are happy to eat fish from even the smallest pond.

However, ponds do need maintenance to prevent the increase of algae and decaying matter. Too many dead leaves and other decaying material can cause a build-up of methane, and full sunlight can lead to excessive algal growth. It is important to avoid using chemicals to control water quality; eliminating one link in the pond cycle chain has implications for all the wildlife it supports. It is usually best not to introduce fish into a small wildlife pond as they can deplete the oxygen and add to the organic matter, disturbing the natural balance, and eating the larvae of many invertebrates, the spawn and tadpoles of frogs and toads, and the larvae of newts.

The Plants

Many aquatic insects only need water for one or two stages of their life cycle; commonly eggs and larvae need to be in water, and the adults emerge to live on dry land or take to the air. Dragonflies, damselflies and the China mark moth are all examples of invertebrates that use aquatic plants on which to lay their eggs, which hatch to complete their larval stage in water.

Just as with land plants, aquatic plants confer qualities to their setting, as well as being important to the other creatures that live there. Submerged plants from the algae upwards release oxygen into the water as a result of photosynthesis. They create a habitat and surfaces for the water-living creatures to hunt, eat, hide and grow.

Conditions for plant growth in a pond are favourable, as water is not limited. A nutrient-rich pond can lead to rampant plant growth, overshading and further nutrient release as the plant decomposes (Buczacki, 1986). If a pond could have ambition, it would be to become a woodland. Maintenance of the pond, and preventing excessive organic matter falling into it, holds that process back (Gardeners' World, n.d.).

Rodgersia aesculifolia lining the edge of the lake at University of Bristol Botanic Garden.

As with all planting design, thought must first be given to what effects are wanted and which plants will suit the conditions. Designers should also pay attention to which animals will be drawn to the pond and what their needs are. Submerged and emergent plants create an underwater jungle that provides a variety of conditions for aquatic animals. As well as providing places to hide from predators, or to lurk in wait for prey, plants are often the substrate on which eggs are laid and larvae settle. Emergent plants may provide the means for insects to moult and take to the wing. Frogs can sit within them, half in, half out of the water.

In winter, a pond may seem lifeless, as most invertebrates will be overwintering in the detritus at the bottom, and plants will be dormant. It is in this period that the plants beyond the marginals – ones that associate well with water, but do not actually need to be wet – are most appreciated. *Helleborus*, *Heucherella* and evergreen ferns all provide a frame for a pond edge when most of the marginal planting has retreated underground. In the same zone, but dormant in winter, plants with big leaves – arum lily (and its glamorous relative *Zantedeschia*), *Hostas*, *Bergenia* and *Osmunda regalis* – associate well visually with water.

In the shallows, from which the water may retreat in dry periods, a rich variety of plants thrive, and care must be taken not to introduce those that will overwhelm a small pond. Pond planting is an instance where native is best. The conditions in ponds promote rapid growth, and some introduced plants have become problematic (WWT, n.d.; Gardeners' World, n.d.).

Myosotis scirpioides, one of the plants where newts lay their eggs, is tolerant of the wet margin, and in deep water, *Veronica beccabunga* is an ideal transition plant that bridges the wet margin to the drier zone outside the pond. In deeper water, *Myriophyllum spi-*

Southern Hawker dragonfly laying eggs on old deck timber edge to a pond.

catum oxygenates the water, and its dense growth of delicate fronds accommodates small creatures, eggs and larvae.

In creating shallow edges for the pond, the designer should select marginal plants with roots to stabilize the edges. This planting also creates cover for animals approaching and leaving the water, whether they be birds coming for a drink, frogs and toads, newts and amphibians at the end of their aquatic phase. Open areas of margin are also needed by those birds and bats that swoop in to take water on the wing.

Taller emergent plants, like purple loosestrife and yellow flag iris, create dramatic and attractive effects, as long as they do not dominate the pond, as, while they are actively growing, they absorb oxygen from the water.

Floating plants oxygenate, as well as creating shade in the pond and places for insects to rest, mate or emerge into their adult form. Water that is high in nutrients encourages a flush of the less desirable duckweed, while frogbit and water soldiers grow more slowly, showing their characteristic contrasting forms. All floating plants retreat underwater in winter, which is also the time when the water may be at its clearest, and submerged plants, such as *Myriophyllum spicatum*, are even more important for cover (Gardeners' World, n.d.).

Rain Gardens

Depending on how long since it last rained, and where we live, we may be delighted to see rain, or dismayed. It may be welcome to have the air refreshed and soil irrigated, or disastrous when rain causes flooding, crop destruction and threats to life and livelihoods. Building Regulations in England and Wales have made it compulsory to manage new building run-off within the property boundary wherever possible.

Rain gardens are one way of getting the most use and enjoyment out of water, and ensuring that it can be returned to the ground, rather than into drains. Rain gardens are permanent, but the periods of inundation are temporary. They serve as ornamental soakaways from which we derive pleasure, entertainment and planting opportunities, while meeting the needs of many kinds of insect life. At any stage before disappearing down a drain, stormwater from roofs and hard surfaces may be designed into a sequence in which its progress is delayed, and it ultimately soaks into the ground, is taken up by plants or evaporated. In their book *Rain Gardens*, Nigel Dunnett and Andy Clayden (2007) have explored ways in which water can be managed more sustainably in small-scale landscapes and private gardens.

To merit the description of 'garden' rather than engineering, a rain garden should be attractive, not just in wet weather, and it needs a degree of resilience and flexibility. In making the water visible in its progress between the source – a roof – and its endpoint – the soil – it may animate moving parts such as a waterwheel or a tumbler. Ultimately, it creates an opportunity to grow some moisture-loving plants in different habitats, when having a pond would be unsuitable. Safety is an important consideration, as with all water in a garden, and in rain gardens water is seldom deep enough to be dangerous.

A simple variation on a rain garden may consist of an ornamental tank that overflows into a bog garden. If room permits, a rocky rill could be introduced, which takes water through the garden, but can be an attractive feature when dry, housing plants that tolerate variable conditions. The water reaches a shallow, dished area of ground where it can collect to intermittently flood an area furnished with suitable plants. The rain planters designed by Wendy Allen (*see* photo on page 117) are made from galvanized drinking troughs. They are fed with rainwater from the blue downpipe, slowing the flow and volume of water reaching drains and rivers, and helping to prevent flash flooding and river pollution. Unlike rain gardens, rain planters can be positioned near building foundations to provide valuable planting space.

Calculation of the requisite area for drainage into the soil varies according to the roof area, the soil type and average rainfall (University of Wisconsin, n.d.), and the rain garden may be extended as a linear swale to give more depth and holding capacity. For play, rainwater needs to be collected and stored to be released later in a splashy, catchable way from waterspouts, waterfalls and any other way gravity can be enlisted. While moving water can be enjoyed from a dry viewpoint indoors, it also needs to be accessible to children when it is not raining, and never better than when the weather is hot. Water that is going to be played with should be stored in a cool place out of the sun, and not left warming in a hosepipe, to minimize risk of *Legionella* bacteria accumulating.

Rain planter designed by Wendy Allen as part of a sustainable urban drainage (SuDS) solution for Action for the River Kennet in Wiltshire.
WENDY ALLEN

A rain garden should form a logical component of the design of a garden. As well as the practical considerations of separation from the house, access for maintenance and siting for appreciation, the shape and position need to be integrated. The dished area may be best suited as a crescent surrounding a lawn, where it may make a corridor for insects, or as part of a border, where it merges into more conventional herbaceous planting. The appearance in winter should also be considered.

Growing Conditions

The planted parts of the rain garden are likely to be dry more often than wet. Even moisture-retentive soil will dry out from time to time. The plants chosen must be tolerant of these conditions of drying out and periodic inundation.

Plants that grow naturally at the margins of a pond are suited to these changing circumstances and are a good place to start looking. There are also many garden plants that thrive with periodic inundation in these places, though we seldom think of them as marginal plants. *Luzula nivea*, *Persicaria affinis* 'Superba' (semi-evergreen), *Rogersia*, *Astilbe*, *Alchemilla mollis*, *Ligularia*, *Lythrum salicaria* and many varieties of *Hemerocallis* are amongst them. Not all of these are good food sources for wildlife, but they do provide shelter. Further planting suggestions and advice are contained in the *Rain Garden Guide* (Bray *et al.*, 2021).

It is desirable to maintain winter structure and interest in marginal planting. Evergreen plants are less inclined to survive standing in water through the winter, but certain sedges, including *Carex elala* 'Aurea', hold their leaves through the winter, and *Helleborus* and *Phyllitis scolopendrium* will grow where their roots are not continuously wet.

Suitable large shrubs include *Salix rosmarinifolia*, with its rusty brown twigs exposed in winter, and *Cornus sanguinea*, with red stems, best placed where they catch the winter sun. Both are suitable for damp places in small gardens and tolerant of pruning. Common elder makes a small tree, spectacular in spring with its heads of sweetly scented white flowers followed by black berries, and also tolerates periods of flood and drought. Other willows, poplars and alders are all suited to the conditions, where space allows.

Up Close and Personal

A garden pond will provide hours of pleasure, both active and resting, and a seat within the pond setting to

Gently rising decking over water, bringing people close to the dense aquatic planting in the Bloedel Reserve in Seattle, Washington.

observe its wildlife is a very welcome feature. Including a quiet, secluded space in the design – perhaps a small area of decking – where humans can be contemplative and peaceful, stills the mind and also encourages animals and birds to approach the pond without fear.

Bridges, jetties and boardwalks allow us to get close to the water, and to look directly down into it, but may be impractical for the average garden pond. A place to lie close to the edge gives a different view of underwater life, which can absorb a curious observer for hours.

Crossing the Water

Mien Ruys was a modernist designer whose work can still be seen at her gardens in Dedemsvaart in the Netherlands. The Marsh Garden, one of her final designs, was built in 1990 (Tuinen Mien Ruys, 2013). The pond is unashamedly rectilinear, framed with a line of vertical posts, a linear edge of decking and square stepping stones – all made from recycled plastic. There is an interplay of textures, forms and colours in the exuberant planting that reaches up above visitors' heads and flops over the edges of the pond. An existing hedge of *Acer campestre* encloses the south side of the garden and opposite there are several mature *Salix alba*.

Steps meandering across a pond, creating shaded areas of water as well as a crossing in this garden designed by Mien Ruys.

Along one edge, the ground slopes gradually to the water, providing places for creatures to gain access, while sheltered by the vegetation. There is also a sense of seclusion for the human visitors who have to cross the pond one by one on the 'floating' stepping stones. Enveloped by planting, they can pause and quietly watch the reflections and pond life surrounding them.

'Ruban Rouge', an installation by Kongjian Yu of painted bamboos beside a timber path crossing wetland designed to accommodate periodic flooding at the Jardins de Chaumont-sur-Loire.

A shallow rill passing over stone slabs and blocks of naturalistic planting tolerant of occasional flooding, commingled with white granite blocks. Designed by Ulf Nordfell for Chelsea Flower Show 2009.

Much of the pleasure that water in the garden provides comes from the creatures that make use of it. While the animals are busy, we are encouraged to slow down, watch and reflect, and we are soothed by the sounds and the sight of water. A well-designed water feature rewards the designer out of all proportion to the space it occupies in the garden, being a magnet for wildlife, an attraction to the human garden occupants and an invitation to unwind.

Design Tips

- Wildlife does not mind if ponds are formal or rectilinear, as long as access is considered.
- Create a variety of habitats in a pond with different levels and edge treatments.
- Bear in mind the potential for reflections.
- A shallow water bowl attracts birds and can be a focal point in the design.
- Match plant vigour to the size of the pond.

CHAPTER 8

PLANTING DESIGN TECHNIQUES

When designing with plants, we are taught to focus on forms: the shape and habit of a shrub; its horizontal or vertical presence; the outline of flowers; the size of leaves. The designer creates visual interest in the way they use these attributes in groupings – in the combinations, contrasts and repetitions. In horticulture, traditionally, gardeners were taught to treat plants individually, providing each one with the optimum conditions and maintenance to ensure perfect flowers or the best crop of fruit. When designing habitats, we must think differently; rather than creating structure and beauty through discrete combinations of individuals, the focus must be on groups, on a mosaic of plants. (We use the term mosaic to describe the intermingling of plants and vegetation in a particular area, rather than the ecological usage where a mosaic is a mixture of habitats, some of which may be of limited use for wildlife, such as agricultural monocultures.) However, without structure and form the garden risks being seen as an undifferentiated homogeneous mass. When designing to create habitats, it is still important to consider such things as the views from the house and the seating areas, how the eye is taken around the garden, the focal points, the aesthetics, seasonal interest – in other words, the human perspective. In this chapter, we consider how this can be achieved, the ways in which by designing mosaics, and thus habitats, we can create visual and sensory relationships between spatial and temporal patterns and processes.

Layers

It is through the planting design that we can introduce the different spatial layers discussed in Chapter 3. Retaining existing trees ensures that there is a ready-made canopy at a reasonable height, which can be enhanced by the addition of other trees in the form of saplings or half standards. In a small garden, if the mature tree is casting shade, learn from nature and select plants that grow in woodland or at the woodland edge, such as rowan, hazel, field maple, hawthorn and crab apple. Multi-stemmed trees form a transition between the canopy and the shrub layer. Taller herbaceous plants and large grasses can also be chosen to occupy the middle zone and these in turn merge with the field and ground layers, which include clump-forming perennials and semi-transparent grasses, low-growing prostrate and mat-forming shrubs, together with winding and scrambling plants. Stress-tolerant species perform better in these conditions, as they may be shaded for parts of the year. It can also be useful to think of an underground layer made up of bulbs, corms, tubers and fungi. Finally, there is another transition layer – the climbers – which, depending on their vigour, extend up into the canopy.

Structure is created through the system of layers using anchors, punctuation and framing devices. It is helpful to use weaving as an analogy – the structure-providing elements and the spatial layering can be thought of as the warp (the thread that is initially strung over a loom and holds the tension whilst weaving) and the more dynamic and ephemeral planting is the weft (it weaves through, under and over the warp). Using the concept of weaving enables designers to create planting schemes that are dynamic, ephemeral and changing, as well as constant. They are designed in a purposeful manner but also leave open the possibility of chance, of self-seeding, of opportunism, and even of messiness and disorder.

Weaving – the Warp

When designing a planting mosaic it is usually easiest to start with the canopy and understorey: these form the main structure of the garden and provide different habitats for shelter and food. In smaller gardens, there may only be room for a small tree, or two or three larger shrubs, but these can still contribute to a range of habitats. Trees that can be coppiced or pollarded, forming the transitional layer, may be a suitable choice for small spaces, and there may also be trees and shrubs beyond the boundaries that can form an extension of the mosaic.

If the garden is larger, there is an opportunity to introduce several trees and layers of shrubs of differing heights and forms. As we have pointed out previously, it is important to use the 'as found' approach and to consider the habitats that already exist. Try to retain trees and to weave the new planting around them.

Although it may be years before a hedge, shrub or tree reaches a reasonable size, it is essential to allow space for this growth. There is little point in creating a habitat with plants that will outgrow the space fairly quickly and need constant pruning or even removing. In order for a hedge to provide useful shelter, protection and nesting sites, it needs to be tall and wide: anything under a metre in width is probably too narrow. However, the design could specify that a section of hedge be left to grow taller, while the remainder is clipped to a more formal shape. In order to avoid leaving areas of bare soil when waiting for a hedge or tree to grow, annuals, bulbs or perennials can be seeded or planted beneath.

Anchors

Within the spatial layers, plants are chosen to anchor the composition in place. These are not necessarily focal points (although they could be), rather they are static forms around which other planting can flow. Shrubs and trees are the most likely choices for anchoring devices but tall grasses with a strong form even in winter, such as *Miscanthus*, could also be used. In a small garden, multi-stemmed and coppiced trees serve as anchors: *Osmanthus aquifolium* and *heterophyllus* and *Corylus avellana* are good examples. In the plan of the warp for the South London garden pictured (page 125), the avenue of *Betula pendula* continues beyond the plan, along the side of the house to the east, forming a strong anchoring structure. Multi-stemmed *Amelanchier lamarckii* also anchors the design, creating a transition between the mid-shrub and canopy layers. Other anchors contribute to the middle layers, except for *Helleborus argutifolius*, which mingles with the field layer of weft planting.

Fruit trees also anchor the ground and field layers – the quince is particularly attractive. One design technique is to arrange them on a regular grid with meadow or naturalistic perennial plants flowing and weaving beneath their branches – a perfect example of the warp and weft analogy.

Clipping evergreen anchoring shrubs and blocks of hedging creates contrasts with the dynamic forms and colours of the surrounding plants, forming interesting tensions and juxtapositions between solid, dark mass and light, and ephemeral flower and seed heads. A large evergreen, such as *Choisya*, *Viburnum*, *Elaeagnus × ebbingei* or yew, continues to provide shelter even when kept pruned. These shrubs also provide food for insects and birds, and *Elaeagnus* has sweetly scented flowers that are a delight for human visitors in late autumn. It is important to let some trees and shrubs grow naturally, wherever possible: this ensures a good supply of flowers and berries and maximizes the foliage cover to provide diverse habitats.

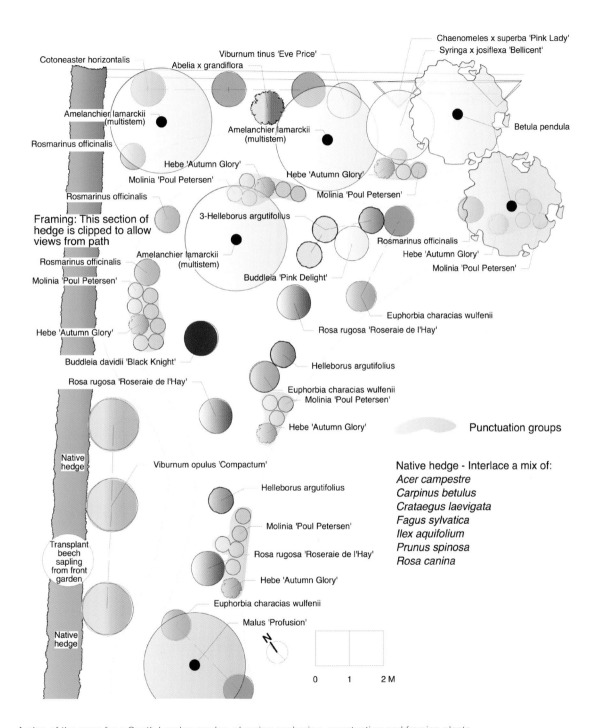

Chaenomeles x superba 'Pink Lady'
Syringa x josiflexa 'Bellicent'
Viburnum tinus 'Eve Price'
Abelia x grandiflora
Cotoneaster horizontalis
Amelanchier lamarckii (multistem)
Rosmarinus officinalis
Amelanchier lamarckii (multistem)
Betula pendula
Rosmarinus officinalis
Hebe 'Autumn Glory'
Molinia 'Poul Petersen'
Hebe 'Autumn Glory'
Molinia 'Poul Petersen'
3-Helleborus argutifolius
Framing: This section of hedge is clipped to allow views from path
Rosmarinus officinalis
Hebe 'Autumn Glory'
Molinia 'Poul Petersen'
Rosmarinus officinalis
Amelanchier lamarckii (multistem)
Molinia 'Poul Petersen'
Buddleia 'Pink Delight'
Hebe 'Autumn Glory'
Euphorbia characias wulfenii
Buddleia davidii 'Black Knight'
Rosa rugosa 'Roseraie de l'Hay'
Rosa rugosa 'Roseraie de l'Hay'
Helleborus argutifolius
Euphorbia characias wulfenii
Molinia 'Poul Petersen'
Hebe 'Autumn Glory'
Punctuation groups
Native hedge
Viburnum opulus 'Compactum'
Native hedge - Interlace a mix of:
Helleborus argutifolius
Acer campestre
Carpinus betulus
Crataegus laevigata
Fagus sylvatica
Ilex aquifolium
Prunus spinosa
Rosa canina
Molinia 'Poul Petersen'
Transplant beech sapling from front garden
Rosa rugosa 'Roseraie de l'Hay'
Hebe 'Autumn Glory'
Euphorbia characias wulfenii
Native hedge
Malus 'Profusion'
N
0 1 2 M

A plan of the warp for a South London garden, showing anchoring, punctuation and framing plants.

A quirkily clipped hawthorn hedge frames the garden beyond.

Mature cedars form anchors surrounded by swathes of mown and long grass.

At Le Jardin Plume in Normandy designers Patrick and Sylvie Quibel have created long vistas of mown grass and bizarrely clipped box hedges to frame an exuberant mass of brightly coloured perennials and grasses.

Punctuation

A second element of the structural warp acts as a form of punctuation around which the planting weaves. These plant groups allow for a breathing point, a pause, a place for the eye to rest in the more random intermingling in the mosaic. Punctuation groups are repeated through the layers creating a rhythm to the design. For example, a combination of low, clipped shrubs, flat-headed *Sedums* and grasses, changes in form and colour with the seasons, while always retaining a structural presence. These pauses are repeated several times among the other planting, and in a larger composition, different varieties of the same species could be incorporated to add interest, while still maintaining the sense of rhythm. The repetition of punctuation groups is the unifying element among the more random planting of the weft. The garden plan of the warp for the South London garden, pictured earlier in the chapter, shows how the repeated punctuation combination of *Hebe* and *Molinia* creates continuity in the field layer.

Framing

In the Preface, we mentioned the importance of cues to care (Nassauer, 1995), to signal that what might appear as merely messy is, in fact, valued and cared for. Cues can be thought of as framing devices. Often these are as simple as a grassy path through a meadow or a mown strip round the edge of a rough, overgrown lawn. However, framing devices are also useful to bring structure to a less ordered planting. Hedges are a good example – they can be winding or geometric, tightly clipped or more overgrown. One way of creating diversity is to have a section of the hedge that is clipped, while leaving another to grow more naturally (an example is shown in the South London garden plan of the warp, pictured earlier in the chapter). If there is space, this can be repeated along the length of the hedge. Or, in larger gardens, one of the hedging plants could be left at intervals to become a tree. Similar to a hedge but in lower shrub and field layers, rows or winding sweeps of *Rosa rugosa*, *Lavandula* 'Hidcote', sage or rosemary, for example, can be used to frame a mosaic of random planting.

Framing plants are also used to signal transitions, edges and even no-go areas. Although designing for habitats does not mean the garden needs to be completely messy, there may be areas that are left to their own devices, where natural succession is encouraged to add to the diversity. Transitions and edges, for example, between a pond and a lawn, can also be thought of as frames and are important areas for wildlife, requiring careful consideration in a design.

Stachys, *Salvia* and *Phlomis* create ripples around anchors of yew at Broughton Grange designed by Tom Stuart-Smith.

A line of vertical posts frame the interlacing planting scheme designed by the late Mein Ruys at her garden in the Netherlands.

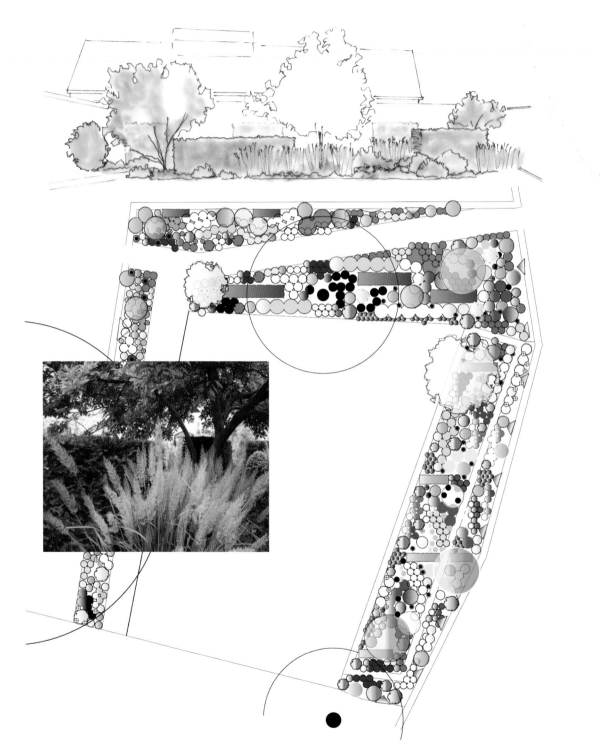

This planting design for an Oxford College uses lines of clipped box and yew to frame the dynamic clusters and ripples of grasses and perennials, chosen for their attractiveness to pollinators.

Weaving – the Weft

Once the structure of the mosaic has been mapped out with the anchoring, punctuation and framing plants, the plants that form the weft are woven in three-dimensional flows and swirls around the remaining space. Four different techniques are discussed here: interlacing, clustering, rippling and chance. Often several techniques are combined in a design, as this will ensure not only a greater diversity, but also result in a dynamic, semi-natural aesthetic. The size of the garden will determine to some extent the choice of technique; it is difficult to create large drifts in a small space, while still introducing a wide range of plants.

The warp and weft are designed to create a mosaic that increases diversity, while also adhering to principles such as unity, balance and rhythm that make the garden aesthetically appealing. Where a traditional planting design is called for, the principles of the warp remain the same but the weft is more likely to include groups of a single plant (clusters). In this case, dotting bulbs and ephemeral plants such as *Aquilegia* and *Digitalis* through the groups, introduces a random element to the design.

Interlacing

The simplest technique, at least on paper, is to do away with a plan and to select a palette of plants in different proportions for a particular area. We call this approach interlacing. Once on site, the contractor or gardener is tasked with planting randomly, resulting in an overall mingling of forms, colours and heights. This approach might appear to be the easiest but has its challenges. The choice and proportion of each plant is crucial, as not only must the designer consider the usual factors such as soil and aspect, but also have an understanding of relative vigour and competitiveness. It is easy over time for one species to dominate and for others to die out completely.

Perennials fall into three broad categories: competitors, tolerators and ruderals (Grime, 2002). In fertile soil, competitors grow strongly becoming large plants that dominate the slower growing stress-tolerators. Adding nutrients benefits the former over the latter; however, the tolerators cope with adverse conditions such as drought, low light levels and poor substrates. *Aquilegia* and foxglove are opportunists; they grow quickly, taking advantage of a patch of bare soil, before seeding, then often dying after a year or two. Ruderals are pioneer plants, found in unstable habitats that are subject to constant or recurring change. Designers can take advantage of this behaviour and select species with the expectation that they will dot themselves around the garden over time. However, it is not sensible to rely on a plant self-seeding consistently; aquilegias are notoriously unpredictable, sometimes surviving several years, occasionally seeding, often disappearing completely. Conversely, in certain conditions, seeding is so successful that the plant begins to dominate the garden.

In the plan of the weft for the South London garden, interlacing is confined to the areas under the anchoring trees. The taller perennials in the sunnier, open spaces merge with these lower growing species that are adapted to semi-shade.

Clustering

Clustering most closely approaches the conventional way of designing. Plants of the same variety are clustered in groups and contrast with a different neighbouring cluster. The clusters then repeat around the planting, adding to the rhythm of the scheme. This technique could be more beneficial to pollinators than an intermingling design; as we pointed out in Chapter 1, Rollings suggests that bees prefer feeding where there is a mass of the same flower in order to get the best possible quantity of nectar. This is an area where more research is needed.

The clustering technique, sometimes combined with interlacing of bulbs or more ephemeral perennials, lends itself to the designing of small gardens. Plants chosen for clusters can also be used as ripples in the same scheme. This is demonstrated in the plan for the weft of the South London garden, where *Aster × frikartii* 'Monch' is used in both clusters and ripples.

Rippling

Creating ripples of planting that flow around the structural elements gives the designer an element of control, although the overall effect appears dynamic. In this case, groups of plants are chosen and repeated in an intertwining pattern. Each ripple can connect or

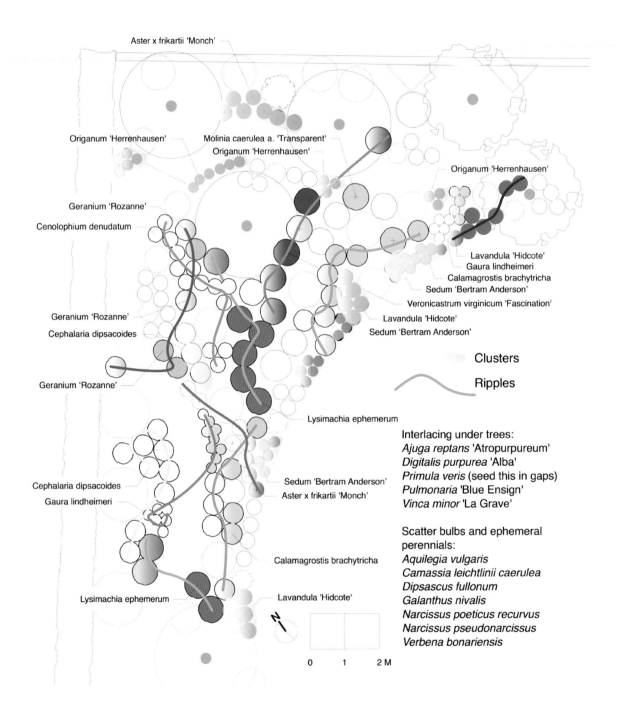

Aster x frikartii 'Monch'

Origanum 'Herrenhausen'

Molinia caerulea a. 'Transparent'
Origanum 'Herrenhausen'

Origanum 'Herrenhausen'

Geranium 'Rozanne'

Cenolophium denudatum

Lavandula 'Hidcote'
Gaura lindheimeri
Calamagrostis brachytricha
Sedum 'Bertram Anderson'
Veronicastrum virginicum 'Fascination'
Lavandula 'Hidcote'
Sedum 'Bertram Anderson'

Geranium 'Rozanne'
Cephalaria dipsacoides

Geranium 'Rozanne'

Clusters

Ripples

Lysimachia ephemerum

Interlacing under trees:
Ajuga reptans 'Atropurpureum'
Digitalis purpurea 'Alba'
Primula veris (seed this in gaps)
Pulmonaria 'Blue Ensign'
Vinca minor 'La Grave'

Cephalaria dipsacoides
Gaura lindheimeri

Sedum 'Bertram Anderson'
Aster x frikartii 'Monch'

Scatter bulbs and ephemeral
perennials:
Aquilegia vulgaris
Camassia leichtlinii caerulea
Dipsascus fullonum
Galanthus nivalis
Narcissus poeticus recurvus
Narcissus pseudonarcissus
Verbena bonariensis

Calamagrostis brachytricha

Lysimachia ephemerum

Lavandula 'Hidcote'

N

0   1   2 M

A plan of the weft for the same South London garden featured earlier, showing the interplay of clusters and ripples and the contrasts between the anchoring trees and the interlacing plants beneath.

An interlacing scheme of *Verbena*, teasel, evening primrose, *Achillea* and *Eryngium* provide pollen, nectar and long-lasting seed heads.

Clusters of *Phlomis*, *Allium*, *Salvia* and *Achillea* combine to create a tapestry of colour in the Great Broad Walk Borders at Kew Gardens, designed by Richard Wildford.

cross over or mingle with others. This is achieved by designing a ripple of five or seven plants that then jumps over an anchor, cluster or another ripple, before terminating with one or two more plants. The plan for the weft of the South London garden shows ripples crossing paths and, in places, the ripples can also be designed to merge into, or run through, an area where the interlacing approach is taken. Rippling is most suitable for larger gardens where the full effect of the combination of trailing and swirling plants in three dimensions can be appreciated.

Chance

If conditions are right, some plants chosen for a particular habitat scheme will self-seed. We will discuss management in Chapter 10, but in allowing plants to naturally disperse, a new element is brought into the design aesthetic. This may or may not be a positive feature of the habitat. Designers who use this approach need an in-depth understanding of how plants might behave on a particular site with its specific soil structure, climate and aspect. As previously mentioned, if one plant comes to dominate, diversity is reduced. Careful choice of the plants in the warp is also important; there is the possibility that ephemeral perennials will seed into those with an open structure, creating a muddled combination that is difficult to maintain.

Seasonal Change

An in-depth understanding of seasonal change underpins all planting design. This is true for traditional planting schemes and even more so when designing for habitat creation. It is not sufficient to rely on evergreens to create year-round interest, designers need an understanding of the phenology of each plant – the sequence of annual changes that take place. In Chapter 6, we discussed the importance of food sources, especially in early spring, late autumn and winter. Designing planting for seasonal succession is also crucial for shelter. In addition to the structural elements, plant combinations should include flowering perennials for spring, summer and autumn, as well as a layer of bulbs for early in the year. In order for these plants to weave together successfully, the designer needs an understanding of how a later flowering species or variety affects an earlier

Ripples of *Stipa tenuissima* weave around clusters of *Coreopsis verticillata* in this design by Judy Pearce and Mary Payne. *Verbascum olympicum* and *Kniphofia* form repeated punctuation points.

ceous layers through the winter, weaving with early flowering snowdrops, crocuses and primroses. Alternatively, select mounds of ground cover – *Epimedium* or ferns – that retain a strong form, even as the leaves are dying. When these dead leaves, stems and flower heads are eventually cut back in late February or early March, the bulbs briefly take centre stage before soft, green, new growth appears and the perennials reassert themselves.

Colour and Scent

It is fortuitous that the very attributes that attract pollinators – flower colour and scent – are also attractive to the people who visit and care for the garden. However, schemes that rely on a limited palette of flowering plants or single colours reduce diversity. Designers should move away from thinking in terms of colour schemes and embrace contrasts. It is important to add many different species to the mosaic; flowering shrubs and tall robust perennials will form part of the warp and smaller or more ephemeral perennials, biennials and bulbs trail through the weft, their flower heads visible as dots and splashes of colour amongst the green.

In the interlacing design of a meadow, this mix of many different colours appears harmonious because flower heads are often small and the green background is the unifying element. When using larger perennials, it may be necessary to avoid too much contrast over a large area; it is still important to think about how the planting design is unified and where the eye can rest. It is helpful that many of the species that are best for wildlife will have less showy flowers and the proportion of green in relation to the colour will be greater and act in the same way as it does in a meadow.

In a larger garden, a harmonious colour theme can be used in small areas and then repeated, unifying the space and creating a calming rhythm. Random dots of interlacing plants winding around these clusters or ripples add diversity but do not overpower in their contrasts.

As we have shown in Chapter 6, the shape of the flower and access to nectar and pollen determine whether a plant is beneficial to wildlife. The design can contrast different flower forms – spires, bobbles, umbels, daisies, cups, trumpets and plumes – as well

one. A spring planting palette might include species that thrive on the woodland-edge or along a hedgerow. These plants will be able to cope later in the year when the taller summer and autumn perennials begin to cast shade.

It is possible to plan for structure and, therefore, shelter and food even in the late winter months through to early spring. Choose plants with strong stems and resilient seed heads, such as *Sedum* and *Astrantia* varieties, *Aster* × *frikartii* 'Monch', *Calamagrostis brachytricha*, *Anemone* × *hybrida* and *Hydrangea* 'Annabelle', that stand in the tall herba-

A narrow path brings the visitor close to the scents and sounds of this planting scheme designed to attract pollinators. The planting ripples vertically between the field and shrub layers.

as colours. In this case, the repeating clusters and ripples can be designed with contrasting flower forms and similar colours. The texture, shape and size of leaves form a background to these colourful contrasts. Anchoring plants are chosen for their structure and year-round form, but their leaf shape is also important. Bold, large leaves and the linear foliage of grasses attract the eye, whereas smaller leafed species are more suitable as a background, perhaps as framing plants. A combination of leaf shapes, rather than colourful flowers, can be used to create the rhythmical punctuation elements in a design.

It is important to create opportunities for the human visitor to get up close amongst the flowers, to be able enjoy the aromas, the colourful details, the sheer mass of planting that creates different atmospheres as the seasons progress. But it is always worth remembering that what to us is a colourful and sensory garden scene, to the wildlife is a means of survival.

Lawns, Grass and Meadows

The ground layer in many gardens is grass and, as we discussed in Chapter 6, the simplest intervention that can be made to create habitats is to allow grass to grow longer and to cut less frequently, allowing daisies and trefoils to flower. In some cases, the main focus of the design is a meadow, as demonstrated in the case study (see Box). However, it is also possible to introduce small areas of meadow into a lawn or to seed wildflowers in gaps in the grass and around the edges. Many companies supply wildflower seed mixes and turf for a range of purposes and situations. Whatever approach is taken, it is important to set expectations; wildflowers do not all germinate successfully or they may do nothing for the first year or so.

A meadow or flowering lawn is an example of the interlacing technique with an element of chance that is amplified as the years progress. Framing is important in these designs; a mown path and an open space in the midst of the meadow are both cues to care and an invitation to wander, pause, sit and experience the insects that will be humming and fluttering around you. Mowing is a design tool to: create a chequerboard of shorter and longer grass; change the route of a path each year or even during the year; play with formal and informal shapes, but consider that the shape of the space, the void, created by mowing needs to be coherent, whether linear or organic.

Take framing up out from the ground layer into the mid and upper zones with hedges and trees; there are

Vertical sleepers frame an interlacing meadow of native flowers with *Allium* 'Purple Sensation' creating the occasional accent.

The Meadow Garden

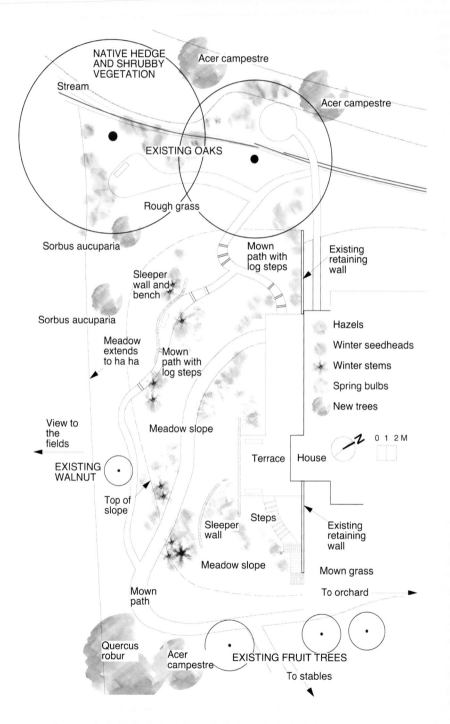

NATIVE HEDGE AND SHRUBBY VEGETATION

Acer campestre

Stream

Acer campestre

EXISTING OAKS

Rough grass

Sorbus aucuparia

Mown path with log steps

Existing retaining wall

Sleeper wall and bench

Sorbus aucuparia

Hazels

Winter seedheads

Meadow extends to ha ha

Mown path with log steps

Winter stems

Spring bulbs

New trees

Meadow slope

View to the fields

Terrace   House

0 1 2 M

EXISTING WALNUT

Top of slope

Steps

Sleeper wall

Existing retaining wall

Meadow slope

Mown grass

Mown path

To orchard

Quercus robur

Acer campestre

EXISTING FRUIT TREES

To stables

Plan of the meadow garden showing winding paths across the slope and areas of perennials, grasses and shrubs to provide structure and cover in the autumn and winter.

(Continued)

(Continued)

When first visiting this extensive site, construction of a new house was underway, including excavation to incorporate a floor below the existing ground level. The spoil had been removed to a distant field, leaving a pile of topsoil and a steep-sided amphitheatre, with a change in level of just over 3 metres. To the west, there were two mature oaks in front of an area of scrub and native hedge that needed attention; and to the east, there were several fruit trees. A small stream ran between the hedge and the oaks. The client wanted to keep the garden simple, informal and open to the expansive views beyond the ha-ha and to ensure that the design blended seamlessly into the landscape of sky, fields, barns and mature trees.

The design enhances the wildlife potential of the site, while creating interesting views from the terrace and the balconies on two floors of the new house. The decision was taken to avoid incorporating any further retaining walls. Instead, the landscape is sculpted into soft curves and mounds with paths, steps and seating areas that bring the clients into close sensory contact with the planting. The garden is a balance of native wildflower meadow, bulbs, mown and rough grass, forming the field and ground layers. The addition of perennials, grasses and shrubs adds colour and winter interest in the field and shrub layers.

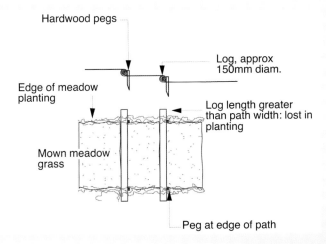

Construction detail of the log steps merging into the meadow planting, creating a transition area for wildlife.

Laying the wildflower turf.

(Continued)

(Continued)

Several native trees have been planted, including some along the hedge line and a small orchard is establishing at the front of the house. Under the oaks and near the stream there is *Corylus avellana*, which will be coppiced. Vertical wooden sleeper walls form the occasional sculptural intervention and serve as framing devices. The new anchors are the two *Sorbus aucuparia* at the top of the slope and the varieties of dogwood – *Cornus alba* 'Kesselringii' and *Cornus sanguinea* 'Midwinter Fire' – within the meadow planting. In the growing season, the shrubs form large clusters of leafy stems providing shelter in the mid layer, but in winter they come into their own as striking anchors of red and yellow stems. Ripples of perennials and grasses, such as *Foeniculum* 'Giant Bronze', *Scutellaria incana*, *Rudbekia fulgida* 'Goldsturm' and *Calamagrostis brachytricha*, also add to the field and tall herbaceous layers, and provide shelter into the spring.

The decision was taken to lay the meadow as a wildflower turf, rather than seeding. This has two main benefits: it establishes immediately, flowering in the first year, and there are fewer problems with weeds, as the whole area is covered with vegetation leaving little bare soil. The turf contains a mix of thirty-four species of native grasses and flowers, with at least 75 per cent wildflowers. In some areas, a mix of bulbs was scattered on the topsoil beneath the turf at a rate of twenty per square metre.

Before laying, the subsoil on the slopes was disturbed with the teeth on the bucket of the digger and then 50–100mm of topsoil was spread over the site. Although a meadow requires low fertility, and sometimes the removal of topsoil, the Wildflower Turf Company who supplied the turf recommended this as a substrate.

The meadow is cut to about 50mm in the autumn after the wildflowers have set and shed their seed. All clippings are removed to ensure that the fertility of the soil remains low. Cutting in this way obviously affects the habitats on the site and removes shelter and food, but if the meadow is left, the rotting vegetation eventually covers the new plant growth and the area will become tussocky. In order to limit the impact on wildlife, cut the meadow in stages and leave a strip uncut around the edge for another month. In this design, there are areas of rough grass, cut in rotation throughout the growing season, that provide cover, and the trees and hedgerow are also important habitats. The seed heads and dying flowers of the ripple plantings remain until early spring, and the new dogwoods will grow quickly to add to the range of habitats for shelter.

The meadow in its first season.

seed mixes for shady areas, as well as sunny. Or focus on the ground and field layers and frame the meadow with water. Again, this can be formal or informal. The long meadow grasses can also create shelter in the transition area between pond and planting, but remember to include some structural planting to provide shelter around the pond in the winter when the meadow is cut down.

Combining Planting and Materials

When designing habitats, the plants and vegetation take centre stage. However, hard landscaping cannot be forgotten: gardens surround buildings and it is important to attract people outside to experience, care for and get up close to wildlife. It is exciting to watch a bee as it works its way around the flower heads in a cluster of perennials or to sit and wait for a damselfly larva to emerge from the pond and gradually transform into an adult. By siting paths and seating areas in positions where they are surrounded by the planting, designers can create these opportunities. Hard surfaces do not need to be impermeable and can contribute to the diversity of habitats in the garden. A gravel path is an ideal substrate for plants to self-seed into; *Helleborus foetidus* – an excellent plant for wildlife because of its early flowering – will take full advantage of the edges where the gravel meets the soil, and gaps in paving can be planted with low-growing, mat-forming perennials.

Pergolas, arches and obelisks provide support for the climbing layer in the spatial structure of the design. These combinations of plant and material can be

Metal poles used as framing devices and to create permeable boundaries at Quai Branly in Paris, designed by Gilles Clément.

Plants for the warp and weft		
Plant name	Wildlife value	Design attributes
Achillea millefolium 'Terracotta' Cultivar of native	Food source for pollinators, including moths.	Feathery grey-green foliage contrasts with bright flowers. Good in clusters or ripples.
Astrantia 'Buckland' and cultivars Non-native	Attracts pollinators, and hoverflies. Seed heads persist through the autumn.	Long-flowering plant for semi-shade. Good as a punctuation plant or in clusters.
Calamagrostis brachytricha Non-native	Long-lasting seed heads provide shelter through the winter into early spring.	Dramatic winter structure with low sunlight shining through dead flower-heads. Good for ripples.
Carpinus betulus Native	Shelter in the canopy and shrub layers. Likely to survive early changes to climate.	Useful for framing as a clipped hedge.
Centaurea montana cultivars Non-native	Food source early in the year, especially for some species of bumble bee.	Colourful flowers. Use in clusters or ripples but will self-seed.
Centranthus ruber Non-native	Good food source for butterflies, moths and bees.	Good for dotting in rocks and drystone walls or in clusters.
Cephalaria dipsacoides Non-native	Good for pollinators.	Pale-yellow flowers above large mounds of deeply cut foliage. Good for clusters and interlacing as part of a semi-transparent tall herbaceous layer.
Ceratostigma willmottianum Non-native	Good for shelter in the field layer.	Late summer, bright blue flowers and seed heads that persist through the winter. Good for low framing.
Cirsium rivulare 'Atropurpureum' Non-native	Good for pollinators	Dots of bright pinkish-purple flowers contrast with green ground cover. Good for interlacing.
Dipsacus fullonum Native	Seed heads remain through the winter as a food source and for shelter.	Sculptural form, good for dotting through ripples of grasses.
Echium vulgare Native	Good for bees, especially bumble bees.	Bright blue flowers for a long period in summer. Works well in interlacing schemes.
Euonymus 'Red Cascade' Cultivar of native	Good for shelter forming a transition between the mid and upper layers.	An anchor with bright autumn colours.
Foeniculum vulgare 'Smokey' Non-native	Seed heads remain through the winter as a food source. Stems provide shelter.	Sculptural form throughout the year. Good as a punctuation plant in the tall herbaceous layer.
Hyssopus officinalis Non-native	Good for pollinators.	Long period of bright blue flowers. Good for interlacing in the field layer and clusters.
Rosa spinosissima Native	Rose hips are high in antioxidants.	Scrambles through hedges or across the ground. Could be trained as an anchoring plant.
Sanguisorba officinalis Native	Good for pollinators.	Delicate semi-transparent layers of flowers above finely cut leaves. Good for ripples.

(Continued)

(Continued)

Plant name	Wildlife value	Design attributes
Sedum 'Autumn Joy' Non-native	Good for bees, but *Sedum spectabile* is the best nectar-producing sedum.	Good as a punctuation or cluster plant. Horizontal flower heads contrast well with vertical grasses.
Sporobolus heterolepis Non-native	Seed heads persist into the winter. Good for shelter.	Light and airy flower heads. Leaves fade to yellow and orange in winter. Good for ripples.
Taxus baccata Native	Evergreen shelter and red fruits.	Can be clipped to create sculptural shapes and formal hedging. Good for framing and as an anchoring plant.
Verbascum cultivars such as *V. chaixii* 'Album' Non-native	Food for moth caterpillars.	Adds vertical accent to planting. Can be used for punctuation and interlacing.
Verbena bonariensis Non-native	A food source, especially for butterflies and moths.	Long flowering period, suitable for dotting around and interlacing. Will self-seed.
Viburnum opulus 'Compactum' Cultivar of native	Bullfinch and mistle thrush like the red berries.	The compact form of the native is a good anchoring plant in smaller gardens.

thought of as anchors in the warp. Similarly, woven willow obelisks with twining clematis or honeysuckle become part of the punctuation. Plant-covered pergolas, walls and fencing play their part in framing, dividing or enclosing different spaces. The supports themselves also become habitats for insects, particularly in winter when little crevices provide shelter.

Sculptural elements also play a part in planting design and can be particularly useful when working with interlacing schemes and those that have an element of chance. A low wall or large pot acts as a framing device or backdrop to ephemeral flowers and seed heads, and has the advantage that it is present throughout the year at times when some dramatic visual interest may be necessary. These too can be designed with habitats in mind; a drystone wall,

pebble-filled gabions or a sculpture of piled slates, all have the potential to become shelter for invertebrates.

Design Tips

- Introduce structure in planting through a system of interconnecting spatial layers.
- Build up a design by weaving clusters and ripples through anchor and punctuation plants.
- Introduce cues to care through framing and mowing.
- Use contrasting leaf shapes and textures.
- Favour plants that will stand through the winter after flowering.

CHAPTER 9

SPECIAL ADDITIONS

In this chapter, we consider the special additions that could be made to a design and that have particular benefits for the flora and fauna of the garden. We begin with a brief examination of the artefacts that can be purchased for inclusion in a wildlife garden. We have kept this section short as there are many websites, books and articles with advice for the garden owner. Instead we turn the focus to the more unusual additions that designers and garden owners might consider, if space and budget allow: green roofs, the traditional techniques of coppicing and pollarding, the use of annuals and the establishing of an orchard.

Wall of found objects providing homes for a range of insects and other small animals.

Artefacts

Throughout this book we have shown how designing habitats in gardens can be done in a subtle and effective way, without the need to accessorize with off-the-shelf artefacts. Nevertheless, it can be advantageous to provide focal points, such as bird feeders, drawing birds in a way that brings them close to us. As with bird boxes and bee hotels, being able to observe animals going about their business is a delight to young and old.

The range of artefacts available to purchase is large: nest boxes, bug houses, feeders, hedgehog houses,

bat boxes, swift and swallow nests and much more. Some of these can be made at home and are a fun way to involve children. However, it is important to ensure that these purpose-built shelter and food stations are sited correctly, otherwise they will fail to attract the creatures for which they are designed. It is also crucial that they are kept clean and do not become a way of passing on parasites and diseases. The solitary bee house shown in the photo at the beginning of this chapter is an example of good practice in this respect. The cocoons can be harvested and protected, any pests can be observed through the viewing windows and it can be taken apart and cleaned each year. Many insect hotels and home-made bug boxes are not suitable for bees, as they attract predators that feed on the eggs and cocoons.

Including artefacts in a garden does not preclude the need for considered habitat design. Feeders must be placed where there is shelter and a safe place for birds to perch and observe their surroundings. Nest boxes are only useful if there is a supply of food for the baby birds and fledglings. Hedgehogs need to be able to roam through different gardens and habitats in search of food and a mate. As with the other habitats in the garden, it is important to educate and set expectations before deciding which artefacts are essential or whether a more integrated solution is possible.

Green Roofs

Specialist advice should be sought before designing and installing a green roof. A structural engineer will assess whether the roof can support the weight of the substrate and plants, and there are companies that specify and supply the roof protection layers and the lightweight growing medium. Waterproofing and drainage need to be taken into consideration, as does the slope of the roof. We do not have the space to discuss these aspects in any depth; however, Dunnett and Kingsbury's book *Planting Green Roofs and Living Walls* (2004) contains a detailed examination of the issues and includes invaluable lists of suitable plants.

Unfortunately, many green roofs, even on new builds, are designed to only support a low-growing sedum mat. If the house or extension is still in the design stage, it may be possible to adjust the roof structure to ensure that it can withstand the weight of a deeper layer of substrate. This gives more possibilities when designing habitats: the deeper the growing medium, the greater the variety of plants that will thrive. However, small-scale green roofs on sheds, log, bike and bin stores can be designed from the outset to bear the weight of 100–150mm of substrate and, therefore, provide opportunities for growing a diverse range of plants.

Choosing plants for green roofs is a somewhat experimental task; they are prone to drought, winds

A Brown Roof Habitat

If the roof is accessed infrequently, and where the aesthetic properties of the vegetation are not a priority, a brown roof is a valuable way to increase the habitats and thus the biodiversity of the garden. Crushed secondary-raw-materials, such as brick and concrete, can be utilized as a substrate, which is left to colonize naturally. These roofs require no irrigation and resemble the open mosaic habitats found on wastelands.

In London, in the second half of the twentieth century, the bomb-damaged derelict sites left after World War II were attractive to the rare black redstart and numbers began to increase. As these sites are redeveloped, and habitats threatened, brown roofs have become a way to support the birds, as well as other invertebrates that favour these habitats (Gedge, 2020). Using crushed materials from the original site as the growing medium is sustainable and benefits the wildlife.

It is unlikely that a brown roof on an extension or loft conversion will attract the black redstart but it is a way of introducing a different habitat from those present in the garden, and it can also benefit from some degree of design input. Creating contours with shallow, sloping mounds and deeper substrates extends the choice of plants and provides visual interest. Research has found that crushed brick and concrete – 25mm-dust – is a suitable growing medium, and this can then be mixed with sand and compacted to create mounds of around 150mm in height (blackredstarts.org.uk, n.d.). Low log piles and larger boulders of waste concrete and stones can also be incorporated, always remembering to consider the added weight.

desiccate the leaves, sun causes over-heating and they may be subject to cold in winter. They also need to cope with the shallow layers of substrate. One place to start is to look at plants that

An intensive roof garden, with boundaries screened and abundant planting for wildlife designed by Todd Longstaffe-Gowan in collaboration with Amin Taha.

Stipa tenuissima ripples through clusters of low-growing perennials on this roof garden of mixed planting tolerant of occasional drying out.

thrive in dry conditions and on clifftops; silver and grey leafed varieties are adapted to reduce water loss and succulents store water in their leaves. Low-growing species are more likely to thrive, while taller plants will often have stunted growth in rooftop conditions.

The roof systems we are discussing here are known as extensive green roofs: maintenance is carried out on the plants as a group, rather than as individuals. These differ from intensive schemes on roof gardens or balconies where large planters are installed and plants with deeper roots, and even shrubs and small trees, can be accommodated. These gardens in the air have seating areas and irrigation systems and, although they can still provide habitats for small creatures, they are less sustainable than the extensive systems. The depth of substrate determines to some extent whether a roof is extensive or intensive: the latter usually necessitates depths of over 150mm. However, the extensive principles can be applied to planting schemes with a substrate depth of 100–200mm – termed semi-extensive by Dunnett and Kingsbury (2004).

As habitats, green roofs are limited due to their isolation: the ways in which habitats link together – the transitions, edges and corridors – are a crucial part of the garden. There are exceptions, however, and in some countries you can see high-rise apartment blocks with plants on every balcony and covering the whole of the facade, connecting the roof areas and walls with the ground below.

Extensive green roofs can be designed to be accessible and even have areas for seating or perhaps for a beehive. It is possible to create paths through the low mounds of planting and to leave a space, perhaps covered with pebbles, where a low chair could be placed. However, it is essential to consider the weight-bearing issues and to ensure there is no damage to the water-proofing membranes.

In many cases, the roof is designed not only for functional reasons but also to be seen: from below with wispy grasses waving above the parapet, from an adjacent balcony or from a room above. If the roof is not being seeded, it is possible to purchase specialist plant plugs with a root depth of approximately 60mm, which allows designers to create ripples and clusters of plants of varying heights, textures and colours, rather than using an interlacing scheme.

Living Walls

In recent years, living walls have been seen commonly on new, and some old, buildings. These are distinguished from green facades (where climbers are rooted in the ground) and are specialized installations, where plants are rooted in pockets or boxes on a framework (Dunnett and Kingsbury, 2004). In situations where there is not space to plant climbers into the ground, they can be beneficial aesthetically, as well as improving air quality and building insulation. The plants used are necessarily small, planted in close proximity and dependent on intensive and exacting irrigation and feeding. Maintenance is challenging and where the systems are not successful, the walls quickly become unsightly; their value to wildlife is limited to shelter, as the plants used are largely non-flowering evergreens.

It is possible to create more biodiversity-friendly green walls in domestic gardens where opportunities for planting in the ground are limited (BBC Gardener's World Magazine, 2019). With some DIY skills, a tolerance of trial and error and understanding of the special needs of plants in these circumstances, the choice of plants can include ones useful to wildlife, particularly some small annuals and perennials. Irrigation would ideally be from harvested rainwater, occasionally dosed with a weak organic plant feed.

Orchards

It is a hard heart that does not swell at the sight of an orchard in spring, in full bloom, abuzz with pollinating insects, or in summer when the ground is clothed in grass and wild flowers, or the autumn when golden and rosy fruits cluster and fall from the branches, or in winter when the sculptural forms and craggy texture of the bare trees is most obvious. 'Orchards . . . tell the seasons frankly' (Clifford and King, 2006: p.309).

Orchards provide oases of biodiversity as mosaics of microhabitats, providing elements of woodland edge, grassland, mature trees, a rich source of old and rotting wood, and often hedgerows (People's Trust for Endangered Species, n.d.). The traditional standard-grown apple tree is long-lived and supports a wealth of wildlife. Spacing of trees in an orchard creates a mosaic of habitats favouring everything from the woodlice and beetles that devour fallen and dead wood, to the deer that browse the fruit and leaves, and badgers that will eat the fallen apples.

The orchard lends itself to being designed on a grid with mown paths and squares of meadow or naturalistic planting, creating contrasts between the ephemeral perennials and grasses and the more formal, sculptural anchors of the trees themselves. Planting adds to the

An old orchard at Le Jardin Plume, Normandy, with contemporary treatment in the mowing regime, designed by Patrick and Sylvie Quibel.

Orchard History

Apples and pears were introduced by the Romans, but their use declined until the Normans brought with them the knowledge of techniques for growing, grafting and pruning apples and pears, expertise traditionally practised in monasteries (Johnson, 2010). Orchards have occupied an important part of the English diet and economy, especially in the counties of Kent, Sussex, Worcestershire, Gloucestershire and Somerset, since the eleventh century. To a lesser extent, apples were grown in south and eastern Scotland, and South Wales – the Norman influence was not as strong as in England. Of the 2,000 or more varieties recorded in Britain, approximately 150 are available from specialist nurseries, but only about twelve are grown commercially (Clifford and King, 2006; British Apples and Pears, 2021).

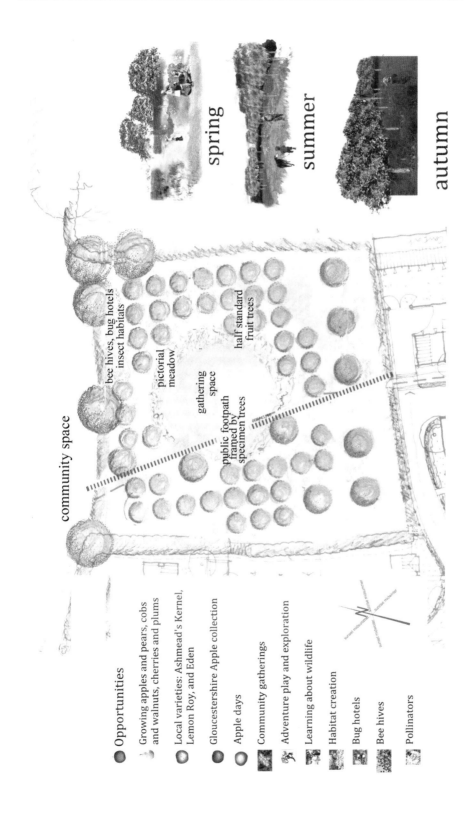

spring

summer

autumn

community space

bee hives, bug hotels insect habitats

pictorial meadow

gathering space

half standard fruit trees

public footpath framed by specimen trees

● Opportunities

Growing apples and pears, cobs and walnuts, cherries and plums

Local varieties: Ashmead's Kernel, Lemon Roy, and Eden

Gloucestershire Apple collection

Apple days

Community gatherings

Adventure play and exploration

Learning about wildlife

Habitat creation

Bug hotels

Bee hives

Pollinators

A plan for a contemporary community orchard.

An informal small orchard in a woodland garden.

Mulberry roof trees make a living pergola over dense mixed planting.

sensory atmosphere and repetition unifies the space and also leads the eye through the trees, along paths and under canopies.

Old wood attached to the tree or fallen to the ground is of particular value to the rare, noble chafer beetle, which is endemic to orchards (Woodland Trust, n.d.-a). Standard apples allow grazing of cattle, sheep and pigs beneath them. Management of the grazing influences the flora of the field layer of vegetation and the vigour of the trees, but modern orchards are more likely to consist of dwarf trees, less imposing in the landscape.

A contemporary interpretation of orchards suited to gardens is the parasol or roof-form tree, with a canopy trained horizontally on trees that respond sympatheti-

cally to pruning. Crab apple, lime (whose leaves are food for many caterpillars), mulberry, *Acer campestre* and *Pyrus* are all commonly found as roof trees. Apples and pears could be grown in a similarly formal way, while still producing flowers and fruit.

In a design, the parasol tree creates a plane of green, bridging the mid and upper layers of the garden. It can give dappled shade over a patio or even be part of a formal planting design, perhaps in combination with ground-cover plants that are happy in light woodland settings.

Roof form and its upright counterpart pleaching, in which trees are trained vertically to a frame, are methods of growing tree canopies in stylized forms, and lend themselves to formal design. Both have the potential to benefit wildlife, depending on the species used.

Pleached hornbeam, like beech, retains its dead leaves when young and when clipped, so provides dense shelter in winter. Pleached trees, or stilt hedges, are frequently created from lime, hornbeam, *Malus*, *Pyrus* and cherry laurel. Like a hedge, they are kept dense by clipping and provide thick shelter, creating a transition layer between the mid and upper layers in the garden, and some provide flowers, fruit and fresh leaves for caterpillars.

Pollards and Coppicing

Many of the ancient trees we see in woodland and as field trees have survived because they have been pollarded in the past. The technique was used to produce crops of wood for poles and firewood, rather than taking the timber from standard trees, used for beams and shipbuilding. The practice is little used now but has applications for design and habitats. In cutting trees back to the same point on a cycle of three to fifteen years, depending on the species and the use, the wood crop is borne at a height out of reach of browsing animals. In woodland, the effect of coppicing (where the branches are cut close to ground level) and pollarding (cutting back to a point higher up the trunk) on a rotation basis – say one-third of trees each year – allows different conditions to prevail

The remains of hedgerow planting resulting in coppiced trees from old wood, soon to be relaid. ALISON GOULDSTONE

A meadow tamed by the framing of pleached trees at The Old Vicarage, East Ruston.

Coppiced woodland and bluebells in Islay, with a natural meandering path where trees meet overhead.

A newly pollarded willow, using a mature tree in the RSPB garden. MARIANNE MAJERUS

through the woodland. Brooks and Follis's (1980) *Woodlands: A Practical Handbook* is a useful source of information.

Coppicing and pollarding have both been practised traditionally on oak, willow, hornbeam, lime, hazel and ash, but there is plenty of scope for the designer to experiment with other trees. Most trees or large shrubs that will shoot from pruning into wood three years old or more, have the potential to coppice or pollard successfully (for example holly but not *Ceanothus*, cherry laurel but not ornamental cherry, and hazel but not witch hazel). In design, the effect of pollarding is to reduce the height of the tree and create a more formal, rounded canopy, whereas a coppiced plant, especially when in leaf, forms a dense mass in the shrub layer.

Shrub dogwoods, such as *Cornus alba* 'Sibirica', are regularly used in design for the winter effect of the colour of their young stems. In order to maintain the production of young stems, the plants are coppiced annually or biannually, and are best planted *en masse*. Willows can be coppiced but are also often pollarded.

Salix 'Britzensis', *S. daphnoides* and *S. capraea* flower with copious pollen in early spring on last year's growth, so it is possible to have both wildlife value this year and prune to get fresh stems that will flower next year. *Salix capraea* is also valuable for its young leaves, which feed many caterpillars, including that of the purple emperor butterfly, and consequently birds (Woodland Trust, n.d.-b). Trees grown now as multi-stems are reminiscent of the coppice form and introduce a sculptural element as they mature.

The annual growth cycle of the species must be understood because it dictates the management of these forms for their potential wildlife value, beyond the density of the crowns, which provide shelter. To repeatedly cut down dogwoods in late winter, to encourage the production of coloured stems, would prevent them ever producing the flowers, useful to pollinators, which only appear on two- (or more) year-old wood. A compromise of cutting to the ground every two or three years ensures a supply of flowers and berries for wildlife. Crab apples produced from

Colourful living willow rods for spiling ridges.

An ancient oak pollard at Staverton Thicks in Suffolk, home to thousands of small plants and animals.

flowers on old stems are promoted by pruning, which encourages fruiting spurs, while pussy willow and hazels produce their pollen-laden catkins on one-year-old growth.

The trunks or stools of these trees age naturally, eventually becoming the gnarled and pitted old wood we see in mature trees, while the canopies are kept in a juvenile state, with constant renewal of shoots. They tend to live longer and lend themselves to spaces such as gardens where they can be limited in size without being disfigured, but this does depend on the training being initiated while the trees are young.

With age, trees develop weaknesses, such as holes, rot and splits, which are beneficial to wildlife but often hazardous to humans. Where it is not safe or desirable to leave dead and dying wood on a tree, removal of a branch and leaving it on the ground is the next best thing, where it can rot with the help of birds, beetles (Piper, 2021) and myriad fungi and detritivores. Again it is not always practical to leave timber lying on the ground, and it may be necessary to log and store it. Log piles are naturally kept by those who want to burn the wood, but it is useful to also have passive log piles of timber that will never be burned, but are allowed to decay, for the benefit of many animals at the bottom of the nutrition hierarchy.

Using Annuals

Designers naturally and rightly take a long-term view of plants, growth and change. In designing soft landscape, the trend is towards shrubs and trees, perennials, meadows and naturalistic planting. Annuals grown from seed, as a meadow in their own right or as a nurse crop, provide colour while a perennial meadow is establishing. There are many seed mixes on the market providing a range of design options and including both native and non-native species. A native meadow usually includes an interlacing scheme of cornfield annuals – *Centaurea cyanus*, *Agrostemma githago*, *Papaver rhoeas* and *Glebionis segetum* – and can establish in places where a perennial meadow will struggle. They are successful when used as a nurse crop with a perennial mix, providing nectar in the first year and helping to suppress weeds. However, they should be cut back and the cuttings removed as soon as they finish flowering (Emorsgate Seeds, n.d.-a): this allows the perennials to develop.

There is still a place for annual plants as part of the garden borders, though the annuals used in traditional bedding have limited value for wildlife. It is helpful to think of annuals as plants that may flower in their first year from seeding. A few of them will go on to flower in a second and third year, and some will not fulfil their first-year potential, but will be strong early flowers in the second spring. As ever, plants do not always conform to the neat categories we place them in.

Annuals have the advantage of a quick reward and a tendency towards serendipitous effects. While the range of annual plants sold in spring is very small, the range available as seed is huge. Most are naturally volunteers – speedy to colonize suitable bare soil – they germinate and grow fast, flower quickly and often exuberantly and set many seeds. Their investment is in securing fast pollination and volume of seed with a limited time to achieve it. They live a much more now-or-never life cycle in contrast with longer lived plants, which build up stores of food and buds. These attributes introduce another element in the development of habitats, as they can provide food and shelter for animals from an early stage.

Annuals such as *Antirrhinum* and *Linaria* require warmth earlier in the year than the British spring usually provides, so may best be started off under glass, but those that do not flower in the first year are sufficiently hardy to overwinter and flower early in their second year. *Cosmos*, *Ageratum* and morning glory (so loved by solitary bees), on the other hand, do not

withstand the winter, so it is necessary to get them to flowering size early in the summer. The traditional method of sowing seeds in pots, pricking out and growing on, gives some certainty and uniformity, allowing for the placing of plants in clusters, ripples and dots.

Sowing seed directly into prepared ground creates a less organized effect and involves more attrition. The large number of seeds in most naturally bred (i.e. not F1) seed packets allows for generous effects, even though some seeds will provide food for birds and other animals (netting may be advisable). *Eschscholzia californica* varieties and other poppies, *Nasturtium*, mignonette and cornflowers all germinate easily and make striking displays with generous quantities of pollen and nectar. Ground-hugging *Limnanthes douglasii* flowers in time for the 'June gap', which beekeepers recognize as a time when there can be a reduction in the availability of nectar in the garden, as spring flowers and tree blossom are spent, and the surge of summer flowers is still to come. *Agastache* and *Monarda* both grow fast into statuesque plants, flowering later in the summer, providing sturdy flowers and dense, long-lasting seed heads standing well into the autumn.

The annuals that become regular self-seeders in the garden can be the most pleasing – *Nigella damascena*, *Echium vulgare*, *Lunaria annua*, *Cerinthe*

Brightly coloured annuals used in naturalistic planting, at the Olympic Park, 2012, designed by James Hitchmough, Nigel Dunnett and Sarah Price.

purpurascens, *Ammi majus*, nasturtiums and *Phacelia tanacetifolia* all have this potential; the annuals that become volunteers will vary from garden to garden and become part of the character of that garden; welcome, but also easy to limit.

Ammi visnaga and *Orlaya grandiflora* are annual umbellifers, providing nectar and pollen for hoverflies, other short-tongued insects and butterflies and

Nicotiana sylvestris and *Ammi majus*, contrasting shapes linked through colour.

moths, which need a position to alight. The wildlife-value that annuals provide is largely in their potential to provide nectar and pollen, but they can also provide cover in summer. The flowers of *Nicotiana alata*, scented at night, attract many British moths, but for generous shelter and shade in summer, and soft detritus in autumn, consider the leaves of *Nicotiana sylvestris* – a 'biennial' that frequently flowers in its first summer.

The pots that play a big part in patio and balcony gardens, densely planted in rich and regularly fed compost, can support abundant mixtures of annuals for pollinators. Single-flowered dahlias, such as 'Bishop of Oxford' and 'Bishop of Llandaff', are not annuals but are on the RHS Plants for Pollinators list (2021d) and have been shown to be a useful addition to the wildlife garden (Garbuzov and Ratnieks, 2014), as is the single annual *Dahlia* 'Bishop's Children'. The bright red *Salvia coccinea*, orange to cream *Calendula* and *Tagetes patula* all contribute to vibrant, fast-growing mixes. Pots are usually emptied and put away at the end of the summer, but could provide shelter throughout the year when some annuals with winter structure are included, perhaps mixed with small evergreen shrubs. *Agastache*, *Lunaria* and teasel, with their persistent structure, provide sculptural interest too.

Design Tips

- Think carefully about where to place artefacts.
- Try to introduce diversity when specifying green roofs.
- Annuals in a design can be useful, but always set expectations.
- Research traditional techniques that could create links with the local area.

CHAPTER 10

MANAGEMENT

Ken Thompson (2007) reminds us that it is not possible to replicate wild landscapes in our gardens. As he points out, habitats such as ancient woodland and meadows are, in fact, the result of centuries of management, rather than examples of unadulterated nature. The habitats in our gardens need different sorts of management.

While the initial design is key to the garden's character, the following years of management should reinforce the design intentions. Designers may not be involved in the development of the garden after the implementation and planting, so it is important to ensure that the client understands the manner and phasing of operations. It may be useful to draw up a schedule with timings, and an understanding of principles is essential. When thinking about management for habitats, these include:

- Ensuring that structure and legibility are maintained.
- Taking a light-touch approach and nurturing change.
- Retaining cover and corridors.
- Focusing on layers.
- Encouraging increasing complexity in the age profile and permeability of planting.

We have emphasized throughout this book that a garden does not have to be wild or unkempt to support wildlife. Formality and orderliness are no barrier to nature, but a lack of density and continuity in space and time would be detrimental. Conventional garden maintenance is often geared towards clear boundaries and visible edges, exposed soil and treating plants as individuals, rather than vegetation. When managing habitat gardens, we need a different approach. However, in creating continuity and joined-up habitats for wildlife, it is still important to protect form and structure in the garden.

The concept of cues to care, which we introduced in the Preface, is helpful; framing key elements of the design ensures that the garden does not become completely overgrown and remains aesthetically pleasing. This may entail: mowing selected areas of grass and meadow; clipping hedges or key shrubs; raising the canopy of trees; ensuring the layout of the design remains legible; training climbers over pergolas and arches; clearing paths and maintaining views through the garden.

Control of Unwelcome Visitors, Pests and Diseases

Some wild and domestic mammals can pose a threat to the wildlife of the garden. Foxes are as brazen in daylight as at night, and though they leave a trail of

A mown path through perennials and long grass shows how the concept of 'cues to care' can become part of the management of the garden, giving structure to more informal areas.

Biological Control

Biological controls for slugs, vine weevil and many lesser pests are widely available, and their effect is to limit pest populations, rather than eliminate them. Biological controls have the great merit of being specific. To kill the whole of a pest population would cause the thinning of their predators as well, leading to a later unchecked surge of the pest population. The target should be diversity of species and balanced self-regulating populations, which is difficult to maintain with chemicals in the long term.

Slugs and snails, whose preference is for young tender plants and cherished species, are some of the most reviled and persistent of garden pests. They thrive on soft vegetation, finding refuge in walls, protected spaces and detritus in gardens. The lack of soil disturbance, which is favoured for other wildlife, favours slugs and snails equally. They are part of the processing of detritus and food for hedgehogs, thrushes and blackbirds.

Codling moth, box moth and some other pests can be controlled by trapping. Hormone traps can be obtained for apple, plum and box trees, where male moths are lured by artificial pheromones of female moths, thereby preventing them from mating and producing the larvae and caterpillars, which do the damage.

Completely eliminating pests and disease is neither practical nor desirable, and cultural control is better to keep species in balance. Avoiding planting uniform species *en masse*, keeping plants appropriately nourished and growing them 'hard' (i.e. not over-watered or overfed), plant hygiene (removing diseased parts) and starting with small plants, which establish better and grow away more strongly, are all measures that contribute to keeping pests at a low level. Throughout the year, 'little and often' is less disruptive than irregular maintenance purges.

destruction, they are as interested in the easy pickings of carrion and food waste as in small animals at ground level. Unfortunately, even hedgehogs can fall prey to foxes. Cats pose a significant threat to birds and small mammals through predation, and the avoidance measures the prey makes to evade capture. Keeping cats in at night and attaching a bell to their collar reduces the kill rate by 80 per cent (Thompson, 2008). Rabbits and deer eat young and mature plants, so some form of protection may be necessary, particularly in the early stages of a garden's development.

Garden plants may not spend their lives entirely unscathed by endemic pests or diseases, but designers should guard against allowing diseased plants to be introduced. Ornamental plants are less attractive to pests than those grown for food. The odd nibbled leaf is unimportant, but to have entire plants razed to the ground, wilted, covered in blackfly or overcome by weeds is dispiriting. Few pests in temperate climates are uniformly destructive, and most are part of a useful food chain, so it is undesirable to completely destroy every member of a pest population.

Chemical solutions are tempting, used under controlled conditions, but there are well-known dangers to wildlife and humans. The most selective and targeted chemicals do least damage to other species. There are a few occasions when specific, non-residual chemicals are useful, such as in preparation for seeding meadows.

Companion Planting

Another way of reducing problems associated with unwanted visitors, particularly when growing vegetables, is to try companion planting. Certain combinations of plants are said to help deter aphids, carrot root fly and other insects. *Calendula* and

Companion planting in raised beds constructed of woven willow.

nasturtium are common examples and yarrow hosts predators such as lacewing, hoverfly and ladybird larvae and thus is beneficial to those plants that are attacked by aphids. Often the companion plant is highly scented and this is meant to confuse the pest. The best results are obtained where the proportion of companion plants is high compared to the plants being protected. They also attract pollinators and may even aid in the uptake of nutrients (Sansone, 2020), although it should be noted that much of the advice on companion planting is based on anecdotal evidence.

Biosecurity

A consequence of the relatively recent trend towards instantly well-furnished gardens is the demand for large specimen plants and semi-mature trees raised in nurseries with softer climates. Designers should guard against allowing diseased plants to be introduced, particularly when imported from abroad. British-grown plants should be specified where possible, and where plants have to be brought from overseas nurseries, biosecurity protocols must be observed. Large specimens are routinely bought from southern Europe, with the highest risk of pathogen import due to the large amount of soil that comes with them, and the wide range of pests and diseases that are potentially imported, coupled with a changing climate with an increased range for some pathogens. Plant passports, which certify that plants have been raised in disease- and pest-free places of production, are required for a growing number of ornamental plants. The guidance on biosecurity is updated regularly and plants that are found to be bearing pests or diseases when delivered should be notified and the appropriate action taken. The Animal and Plant Health Agency (APHA) should be the first port of call if concerns arise about pests and diseases on plants purchased or, indeed, plants established in the garden. Designers should keep up to date with current biosecurity advice, and design and specify accordingly to avoid potential issues. Further information can be found from the website of the APHA (n.d.) and The Arboricultural Association (2021). The Landscape Institute *Biosecurity Toolkit* (2019) is also a useful resource.

Lighting

Twinkling star light on a birch tree adds a subtle, magical touch to the garden at night.

Lighting gardens is undertaken for both practical and aesthetic reasons and can increase enjoyment of the garden into the evening. On the other hand, light shed by lights, especially street lamps, can seem as bright as daylight in some cases and disruptive to humans, just as much as other animals. It is well documented that lighting can also damage the habitats of animals and plants by creating inappropriate conditions for the time of day or season and disrupting behaviour patterns (Russ et al., 2015).

To minimize disturbance to animals in gardens, lighting should be limited to where it is most useful or ornamental. Safety is important, but low levels of light targeted to paths and steps are effective. It is most pleasing when lighting only specific plants or features and when the effect, but not the source of light, is seen – the glow from under leaves, reflecting off water or highlighting a wall, creating shadows. Uplighting with too bright a lamp or too wide a beam can result in light being lost to the sky. It takes very little lighting to make a visual and practical impact in the garden, and too much of it risks blurring the distinction between night and day, in addition to negative ecological effects. Lighting limited in extent and brightness can be more visually exciting than more extensive illumination, and occasional candles can take the place of a generalized functional lighting scheme. During dark winter evenings, it is pleasing to be able to view selected garden features from indoors but, again, this should be kept to a minimum.

The effects of artificial lighting on vegetation outdoors are less obvious, but research shows that not only are the herbivores and pollinators, which depend on plants, affected, so too is the phenology, growth and resource allocation of plants (Bennie et al., 2016).

Nocturnal animals are adapted to be most active and efficient at night and rely on darkness to catch their prey, find mates and raise their young. Bats and hedgehogs are active at night and avoid lit places. The intensity, placing and wavelength of light are all significant to their avoidance behaviour. Detailed information can be found in Voigt et al. (2018). Research continues on the effect of different wavelengths, but it is thought that warm light (K2000–3000) has less impact on bat activity than cool white (K4000–5000, increasingly used in street lighting) (Stone, n.d.). Further mitigation of effects is achieved by narrow beam angles, exclusion of UV wavelengths, directional downlights that are positioned below 2m in height and the lowest effective brightness.

Extensive or Intensive

In all gardens, knowing when to intervene and when to let well alone is a skill that is learned over time by close observation and understanding of the site, the plants and its habitats – and, of course, the preferences of its human visitors. There is no one-size-fits-all solution and, especially when creating and managing habitats, it is important to be clear about what you are trying to achieve. Interference with one area of the garden, or even just cutting back one group of plants, might affect other habitats in the garden and beyond.

With this in mind it is important to consider the difference between intensive and extensive maintenance. We touched on this in Chapter 9 when discussing green roofs. When a whole group of plants is treated in the same way, this is called extensive maintenance, such as all the plants in a meadow (*see* the case study in Chapter 8) are cut back once a year. In contrast, intensive maintenance considers each plant as an individual with its own specific requirements. Traditionally, this entails digging, staking, dead-heading, pruning, weeding, removing seedlings, dividing, fertilizing, watering and more.

Management for habitats is perhaps best thought of as something between these two extremes. And this is where the skill lies. We need to understand when to cut back, which seedlings to leave, how to control unwanted visitors to the garden and, importantly, how to improve the soil.

Scabious and *Sanguisorba* dotted amongst grasses will remain as dried seed heads into the winter months.

Designing with large drifts of perennials calls for a mix of intensive and extensive management. It is on the edges of each drift that competition takes place and a more intensive approach is needed.

Extensive Maintenance and Chance

The garden illustrated (page 158), on a Scottish island, was designed on disturbed land with a clay soil that had been grazed for decades. A house was built on the site and the displaced earth used to contour the levels on the steep slope. The soil is fertile – not the best start for establishing a meadow – and the site is constantly buffeted by salt-laden winds. It is also only possible to undertake sporadic maintenance and, therefore, the garden is almost completely left to chance.

Initially, native trees – rowan, hawthorn and blackthorn – were planted as whips and protected from deer and rabbits. Gorse, cuttings of willow and plugs of yellow flag, loosestrife and meadowsweet were also planted. After sixteen years, many of these are now well established, although, perhaps surprisingly, hawthorn has suffered the most. The bare earth was seeded in places with a native mix of plants, all of which were growing on the island. Some areas of the garden are mowed every few weeks but much is left and only given a full strim in late autumn. There is now a diverse range of habitats, where once there was just closely cropped grass.

An extensive management approach is taken in this Hebridean garden where elements of chance are permitted to modify the original design concept.

Over the years, the mix of vegetation has changed, not only as it matures but also depending on the weather conditions. Some years, amongst the many weeds, docks predominate, in others it is thistles. When thistles and nettles threaten to take over, they are pulled by hand. Sometimes seed heads are removed in an attempt to prevent the spread of weeds, but mainly things are left to their own devices. Many perennials battle with the grasses and weedy vegetation. There are cowslips, ox-eye daisies, knapweed, foxgloves, bedstraws, plantains and a wealth of different vetches, umbellifers and grasses.

However, management through the combination of chance and extensive maintenance is permitting a more natural succession to take place. Brambles, nettles and bracken are all beginning to establish and dominate. After nearly two decades, a more intensive approach may be necessary to reinforce the design intentions and keep the diversity of habitats in some areas of the garden.

Soil and Fertility

We discussed the importance of soil in Chapter 4; indeed, it is a varied habitat in its own right. The composition, structure and pH determines which plants can be grown successfully, and good management can help to improve the soil and the chances of plants thriving.

Leaving plant matter and fallen leaves in some areas of the garden provides shelter and food, espe-cially over the winter. These gradually rot and are pulled underground by earthworms. Compost heaps, piles of leaves and wormeries are also habitats and eventually provide useful fertilizer and mulch for the soil.

The use of fertilizers results in plants growing tall with soft structures that then need staking, and are more appetizing for aphids, slugs and snails. It is better, in a more naturalistic scheme, to avoid artificial fertilizers and to allow plants to support each other and to compete for nutrients. Some may not survive but others will take their place.

The most important way of protecting the soil, improving organic content, retaining moisture, reducing weeds and encouraging plant growth, is to mulch. The RHS (2021a) suggests a wide range of organic mulches: compost, wood chips, bark, leaf mould, well-rotted manure and even seaweed. Green waste compost is also an option. It is most important to avoid using any peat-based composts: you will be destroying a valuable natural habitat. Mulch is applied in a thick layer, at least 7.5cm, in spring or autumn.

No-Dig Gardening

The no-dig method is often advocated in organic gardens and is becoming more common, especially when growing vegetables. In avoiding digging, the habitats in the soil remain intact and the worms and microorganisms, as well as the fungi, are not disturbed. This method uses large quantities of compost

Using Rain Water

In Chapter 7, we discussed how to use the rain falling on our roofs to create rain gardens and even if it is this is not possible, it is still useful to collect rain water in a series of water butts for emergency watering in adverse and unusual conditions, for the years when a plant is establishing, for topping up ponds and for growing vegetables.

It should not be necessary to specify a purpose-built irrigation system for a habitat garden: the concept of 'right plant, right place' should ensure that, after the first year or so, plants will cope with the conditions. If they do not, then maybe they should be allowed to die and be replaced with an alternative. Beth Chatto's gravel garden (Chatto, 1978) in Essex, with one of the lowest rainfalls in the country, is a well-known example of this approach. Before planting, the poor, free-draining soil was improved, and the plants have established with no watering ever since. Some have died, but the resulting garden remains a beautiful example of how to design without resorting to irrigation.

Beside the low water feature there is an unobtrusive pipe that leads through the vegetation to a downpipe, channelling rainwater from the roof to top up the pond.

Planting designed to encompass all the layers in Beth Chatto's gravel garden provides food and shelter for wildlife and is never watered.

or organic matter – a layer of between 15 and 20cm in the first year – laid on some form of light-excluding material, such as cardboard (Garden Organic, 2021). Compost is preferable to something like straw, which can harbour slugs (Dowding, 2018). The cardboard eventually rots down and the natural organisms in the soil gradually help to incorporate mulch into the soil, improving its structure and, over time, perennial weeds, deprived of light, weaken and die. It is sometimes necessary to individually dig out deep-rooted perennials before laying the cardboard and mulch, or afterwards if they still persist. New weeds are hoed off or dug out individually. Seedlings are planted and seeds are sown directly into the com-

post. Surprisingly, this method works on clay soils, as well as those with a more free-draining structure (Dowding, 2018).

When to Intervene

In a garden of habitats, and those with a naturalistic planting aesthetic, the main time for cutting back is in the early spring. This ensures that dead seedheads and stems are left over the winter for food and shelter. The photo at the beginning of this chapter, taken at Bury Court, designed by Christopher Bradley-Hole, reminds us how beauty and form can

Sanguisorba officinalis 'Arnhem' and *Sanguisorba* 'Korean Snow' interlaced with tall *Miscanthus* and other ornamental grasses in this design by Christopher Bradley-Hole at Bury Court.

Dry vegetation left until spring at the University of Bristol Botanic Garden.

be found in planting combinations through the autumn months.

However, there will always be some plants that start to look unattractive as winter progresses and, even with the best intentions, gardeners may want to remove these earlier. If it is essential to cut back, it is possible to shred dry stems and leave them on the ground where they can still provide some shelter.

The temptation to tidy everything at the end of the autumn should be resisted. Rotting fruit under a tree is a food source for birds, small mammals and invertebrates. Leaving grasses uncut can benefit butterflies, such as the orange tip and green-veined white, which overwinter as chrysalides on stems, and large skipper and ringlet caterpillars also shelter in the field layer during the winter (Aylward, 2021).

Grass, fennel and teasel seeds provide food for birds and fallen leaves are places for invertebrates, and even hedgehogs, to shelter. Removing leaves from the lawn (and making leaf mould), but leaving them to gradually rot down in the beds, is a good compromise in the habitat garden.

Weeds, Self-Seeders and Spreaders

When is a weed not a weed? When it is perceived as an asset to the garden. Perhaps it is useful to think of a weed as a plant in the wrong place.

We have discussed competition between plants in preceding chapters, balancing their vigour and allowing succession. Like pests, weeds are unlikely to be eliminated by cultural means – although we have mentioned the success of the no-dig method above – and there are circumstances when it may be useful to clear a site with a selective non-residual herbicide. Herbicides are particularly helpful in clearing ground before seeding meadows, and most effective when there is time for more than one dose to deal with a second flush of emerging weeds.

We saw in Chapter 9 that annuals may establish themselves in gardens where conditions suit them and self-seed in successive years. Seed heads are usually attractive and an asset in providing food and shelter for small animals, but not all are problem-free – dandelion clocks, for instance, though they are loved by children and goldfinches alike. Annuals, whether favourites or weeds, are not difficult to remove by hoe or by hand, but perennials have storage roots of one sort or another, which must be dug out.

Pruning

Pruning is an essential activity for the gardener but, again, it is important to know when and to what extent to intervene. The form of many trees will be lost if they are pruned drastically, and it may be more useful to judiciously raise the canopy to let more light in beneath

Best grown as an annual, the seed heads of *Agastache* provide food and shelter as well as structure to the winter garden.

The dramatic form of a thistle head stands through the winter months.

rather than to restrict the height. In Chapter 9, we also discussed the advantages of coppicing and pollarding, both to the flora and fauna and within a design. Another traditional technique is that of laying hedges; this eventually creates a dense wildlife habitat, while also helping to regenerate the hedgerow. However, there can be a period when the vegetation at the base of the laid hedge is minimal, resulting in a loss of the wildlife corridor (Warner, n.d.).

As we have shown throughout this book, in order to encourage wildlife, a garden needs to be designed with layers of vegetation, and the denser the better. Although shrubs and hedges may need to be cut back to keep them within bounds, if possible, try to leave some unpruned, especially over the winter months. This ensures there are plenty of hips, haws and other fruit for hungry creatures, and the contrast between a

As this photo demonstrates, it is possible to rejuvenate fairly mature trees by laying.

neatly clipped dome or ball and a wilder more dynamic form can enhance the aesthetic of the garden.

Climbers, roses, wall shrubs and fruit trees also require judicious pruning, both to keep them from growing too large and in order to provide a display of flowers and a crop of fruit the following year. It may be necessary to make compromises and to try to leave some hips, berries and seed heads, or at least to leave them as long as possible, but the health of the plant should be the deciding factor. It is important for the long-term development of your habitats to ensure that the plant produces new growth, leaves and flowers in the following years.

Succession

We discussed succession in ecological terms in Chapter 1 and mentioned seasonal change in Chapter 8; however, it is worth looking again at how succession might be approached in the management of garden habitats. All gardens change as they mature, and keen gardeners are always tweaking and intervening. We might encourage self-seeding for a few years and then decide that these seeded species are dominating the perennials and need controlling. Habitats also change: log piles rot down, leaves are drawn into the earth, shrubs and trees mature, ponds are taken over by vegetation. It is clear that creating a garden of habitats is a skilled process. The designer needs to set expectations and to discuss how the garden might evolve over the years, and when and whether it is necessary to intervene. Often these decisions will change: time, money, preferences, priorities and so on, will all determine how the garden evolves. Obviously, it is beneficial if some habitats are allowed to mature – trees, shrubs and hedges, for example. But in other cases, it may be useful to make changes and introduce new plants. The conditions within and outside the garden are not static: a maturing tree begins to cast more

Dermot Foley's Bridgefoot Street Park is beginning to be colonized by garden escapes, including vegetables such as chard, indigenous and ruderal species. Management controls some more aggressive weeds such as fat hen, but the intention is to take a light touch approach.
PAUL TIERNEY

A view of the RSPB garden encompasses areas under different forms management: limited succession under trees, pollarding, self-seeding of perennials, intensive maintenance of perennials and grasses in the foreground and extensive maintenance of the meadow in the background. MARIANNE MAJERUS

shade or a neighbouring one is cut down bringing in more light.

In natural landscapes, some species die and others take their place. In gardens we can make the decision about which plants to remove and which will make good replacements. We do not need to make drastic whole-scale changes, such as might be seen in nature when storm damage or flooding creates new possibilities. Management of garden habitats is about observation and light-touch intervention, little and often.

Design Tips

- Plan for increasing complexity.
- Encourage a light touch approach, little and often is best.
- Avoid the use of pesticides and chemicals and never use peat-based compost.
- Design for a mix of extensive and intensive maintenance.

AFTERWORD

The theme of connectivity has permeated this book. We have stressed the need for linking habitats through layers of vegetation, edges and seasons and that the connections should reach out beyond the boundaries. Neighbouring gardens, hedges, waterways and railway cuttings are all places where corridors exist and can be embraced.

We need to connect with the future. That starts with disturbing as little as possible of the present. The future of the earth in the face of the climate emergency is precarious, but the vast area of gardens in Britain can contribute to carbon absorption, buffering temperatures and soaking up stormwater, and in doing so, give biodiversity a chance. It is clear that water, soil and air will be affected, and while we have little control individually, gardens will have a role in ameliorating adverse local conditions and promoting a healthy atmosphere.

None of this is inconsistent with good design and the opportunity to create a strong sense of place. The needs of plants give clues to the character of the gardens we can create and the habitats that are possible within them. Habitats can be created as readily within formal and contemporary gardens, where the plant choice is thoughtful, varied and abundant, as in the informal and traditional.

We have confined ourselves to discussing private gardens, but allotments and community gardens are equally places that can support wildlife and bring people together in a common aim, at a time when, individually, we may feel powerless. It is always worth doing something to support wildlife; however small the contribution, it will be another link to the natural world.

BIBLIOGRAPHY

APHA (n.d.) *Animal & Plant Health Agency*. Online, GOV.UK. Available from: https://www.gov.uk/government/organizations/animal-and-plant-health-agency [accessed 18/10/2021].

Appleton, J. (1996) *The Experience of Landscape*, revised edition. UK: John Wiley and Sons.

Aylward, S. (2021) Beguiling butterflies. *Wild Suffolk*, Spring/summer, pp. 32–35.

BBC Gardener's World Magazine (2019) *How to Create a Living Wall*. Online, Gardener's World. Available from: https://www.gardenersworld.com/how-to/diy/how-to-create-a-living-wall/ [accessed 7/10/2021].

BBC Radio 4 (2021) *More or Less: Delta Cases, Blue Tits and that One-in-Two Cancer Claim*. BBC iPlayer: BBC.

Bennie, J., Davies, T. W., Cruse, D. & Gaston, K. J. (2016) Ecological effects of artificial light at night on wild plants. *Journal of Ecology*, 104 (3), pp. 611–620.

blackredstarts.org.uk (n.d.) *Green Roofs & Brownfield Biodiversity*. Online, blackredstarts.org.uk. Available from: https://www.blackredstarts.org.uk/pages/greenroof.html [accessed 8/8/2021].

Bostock, H. & Salisbury, A. (2019) *RHS Plants for Bugs – Bulletin 3*. Online, RHS. Available from: https://www.rhs.org.uk/science/pdf/conservation-and-biodiversity/wildlife/Plants-for-Bugs-Bulletin-3-Gardens-as-habitats-for.pdf [accessed 18/3/2021].

Bray, B., Gedge, D., Grant, G. & Leuthvilay, L. (2021) *Rain Garden Guide*. Online, raingardens.info. Available from: https://raingardens.info/wp-content/uploads/2012/07/UKRainGarden-Guide.pdf [accessed 29/6/2021].

British Apples and Pears (2021) *A Brief History of Apples in the UK*. Online, British Apples and Pears. Available from: https://britishapplesandpears.co.uk/about/a-brief-history-of-apples-in-the-uk/ [accessed 10/4/2021].

Brooks, A. & Follis, A. (1980) *Woodlands: A Practical Handbook*. UK: British Trust for Conservation Volunteers.

Buczacki, S. (1986) *Ground Rules for Gardeners*. London: William Collins Sons and Co. Ltd.

Buglife (n.d.-a) *Brownfields*. Online, Buglife. Available from: https://www.buglife.org.uk/resources/habitat-hub/brownfield-hub/ [accessed 22/6/2021].

Buglife (n.d.-b) *Identifying Open Mosaic Habitat*. Online, Buglife. Available from: https://cdn.buglife.org.uk/2020/01/Identifying-open-mosaic-habitat.pdf [accessed 22/6/2021].

Butterfly Conservation (n.d.-a) *Caterpillar Foodplants*. Online, Butterfly conservation. Available from: https://butterfly-conservation.org/moths/why-moths-matter/about-moths/caterpillar-foodplants [accessed 6/4/2021].

Butterfly Conservation (n.d.-b) *Caterpillar Foodplants: Butterflies*. Online, Butterfly conservation. Available from: https://butterfly-conservation.org/sites/default/files/butterflyfoodplants.pdf [accessed 6/4/2021].

Butterfly Conservation (n.d.-c) *Caterpillars – a Brief Guide*. Online, Butterfly conservation. Available from: https://butterfly-conservation.org/sites/default/files/caterpillars—a-brief-guide_leaflet.pdf [accessed 6/4/2021].

Butterfly Conservation (n.d.-d) *Garden Moths*. Online, Butterfly conservation. Available from: https://butterfly-conservation.org/sites/default/files/garden-moths-leaflet-a5-10pp-aw-march-2015-final.pdf [accessed 6/4/2021].

Butterfly Conservation (n.d.-e) *Gardening for Butterflies*. Online, Butterfly conservation. Available from: https://butterfly-conservation.org/how-you-can-help/get-involved/gardening/gardening-for-butterflies [accessed 6/4/2021].

Butterfly Conservation (n.d.-f) *Lives of Moths*. Online, Butterfly conservation. Available from: https://butterfly-conservation.org/sites/default/files/lives_of_moths-factsheet.pdf [accessed 6/4/2021].

Butterfly Conservation (n.d.-g) *Nectar Plants for Moths*. Online, Butterfly conservation. Available from: https://butterfly-conservation.org/sites/default/files/mothnectar.pdf [accessed 6/4/2021].

Cameron, R., Brindley, P., Mears, M., McEwan, K., Ferguson, F., Sheffield, D., Jorgensen, A., Riley, J., Goodrick, J., Ballard, L. & Richardson, M. (2020) Where the wild things are! Do urban green spaces with greater avian biodiversity promote more positive emotions in humans? *Urban Ecosystems*, 23 (2), pp.301–317.

Cardinale, B. J., Matulich, K. L., Hooper, D. U., Byrnes, J. E., Duffy, E., Gamfeldt, L., Balvanera, P., O'Connor, M. I. & Gonzalez, A. (2011) The functional role of producer diversity in ecosystems. *American Journal of Botany*, 98 (3), pp. 572–592.

Ceballos, G., Ehrlich, P. R. & Dirzo, R. (2017) Biological annihilation via the ongoing sixth mass extinction signaled by vertebrate population losses and declines. *Proceedings of the National Academy of Sciences*, 114 (30), pp. E6089–E6096.

Chatto, B. (1978) *The Dry Garden*. London: Weidenfeld & Nicholson.

Clifford, S. & King, A. (2006) *England in Particular: A Celebration of the Commonplace, the Local, the Vernacular and the Distinctive*. Great Britain: Hodder and Stoughton.

Davis, B. (1987) *The Gardeners Illustrated Encyclopedia of Trees and Shrubs*. Great Britain: Viking.

Dowding, C. (2018) *Organic Gardening: The Natural No-Dig Way*. Cambridge: Green Books.

Dunnett, N. & Clayden, A. (2007) *Rain Gardens: Managing Water Sustainably in the Garden and Designed Landscape*. USA: Timber Press.

Dunnett, N. & Kingsbury, N. (2004) *Planting Green Roofs and Living Walls*. Cambridge: Timber Press.

Emorsgate Seeds (n.d.-a) *Cornfield Annuals as Nurse Cover*. Online, Emorsgate Seeds. Available from: https://wildseed.co.uk/page/cornfield-annuals-as-nurse-cover [accessed 15/9/2021].

Emorsgate Seeds (n.d.-b) *Growing Medium: Soils or Soil Substitutes*. Online, Emorsgate Seeds. Available from: https://wildseed.co.uk/page/preparation-and-construction [accessed 27/7/2021].

Foley, D. (2021) Small imperfections – a case study. In: C. Heatherington (ed.) *Revealing Change in Cultural Landscapes: Material, Spatial and Ecological Considerations*. Abingdon and New York: Routledge, pp. 205–217.

Garbuzov, M. & Ratnieks, F. L. W. (2014) Quantifying variation among garden plants in attractiveness to bees and other flower-visiting insects. *Functional Ecology*, 28 (2), pp. 364–374.

Garden Organic (2021) *The No-Dig Method*. Online, Garden Organic. Available from: https://www.gardenorganic.org.uk/no-dig-method [accessed 12/10/2021].

Gardeners' World (2019) *10 Berried Plants for Birds*. Online, Gardeners' World. Available from: https://www.gardenersworld.com/plants/10-berried-plants-for-birds/ [accessed 6/4/2021].

Gardeners' World (n.d.) *Native Pond Plants*. Online, Gardeners' World. Available from: https://www.gardenersworld.com/plants/native-plants-for-wildlife-ponds/ [accessed 16/5/2021].

Gaston, K. J., Smith, R. M., Thompson, K. & Warren, P. H. (2005) Urban domestic gardens (II): experimental tests of methods for increasing biodiversity. *Biodiversity & Conservation*, 14 (2), pp. 395–413.

Gedge, D. (2020) *Black Redstarts, a Story of Renewal – Green Roof Birds 1*. Online, Dusty Gedge. Available from: https://dustygedge.co.uk/index.php/birds/black-redstarts-a-story-of-renewal-green-roof-birds-1/ [accessed 8/8/2021].

Gilbert, O. (1989) *Ecology of Urban Habitats*. London: Chapman and Hall.

Gilmartin, E. (2021) *What is a Root Protection Area and What Does It Mean?* Online, The Woodland Trust. Available from: https://www.woodlandtrust.org.uk/blog/2021/04/root-protection-areas/ [accessed 8/8/2021].

Goulson, D. (2020) Honey Traps. *Garden Design Journal*, November, pp. 21–24.

Grime, J. P. (2002) *Plant Strategies and Vegetation Processes*. Chichester: John Wiley.

Heatherington, C. (2021) *Revealing Change in Cultural Landscapes: Material, Spatial and Ecological Considerations*. Abingdon and New York: Routledge.

Heatherington, C. & Sargeant, J. (2005) *A New Naturalism*. Chichester: Packard Publishing Ltd.

Hitchmough, J. (2020) *Thinking the Unthinkable: Designing with Plants in an Era of Rapid Climate Change*. Online: SGD Digital Autumn Conference 2020.

Johnson, H. (2010) *The Traditional British Orchard*. Online, Building Conservation. Available from: https://www.buildingconservation.com/articles/traditional-orchards/traditional-orchards.htm [accessed 11/4/2021].

Kaplan, R. & Kaplan, S. (1989) *The Experience of Nature*. New York: Cambridge University Press.

Kingsbury, N. (2013) *Clump or Mingle?* Online, Thinking Gardens. Available from: https://thinkinggardens.co.uk/articles/clump-or-mingle-by-noel-kingsbury/ [accessed 7/4/2021].

Kingsbury, N. (2019) Competition time. *The Plantsman*, March, pp. 30–15.

Landscape Institute (2019) *Biosecurity Toolkit for Landscape Consultants*. Online, Landscape Institute. Available from: https://www.landscapeinstitute.org/technical/plant-biosecurity-group/ [accessed 10/10/2021].

Lopez, B. (2020) *Horizon*. London: Vintage.

Nassauer, J. (1995) Messy ecosystems, orderly frames. *Landscape Journal*, 14 (2), pp. 161–170.

Pattrick, J. G., Symington, H., Federle, W. & Glover, B. (2020) The mechanics of nectar offloading in the bumblebee *Bombus terrestris* and implications for optimal concentrations during nectar foraging. *Journal of the Royal Society Interface*, 17 (162).

People's Trust for Endangered Species (n.d.) *Orchard Habitat*. Online, People's Trust for Endangered Species. Available from: https://ptes.org/campaigns/traditional-orchard-project/orchard-biodiversity/orchard-habitat/ [accessed 10/4/2021].

Phillips, R. (1978) *Trees in Britain, Europe and North America*. UK: Pan Books Ltd.

Pinto-Rodrigues, A. (2021) *Bee Population Steady in Dutch Cities Thanks to Pollinator Strategy*. Online, The Guardian. Available from: https://www.theguardian.com/environment/2021/apr/27/bee-population-steady-dutch-cities-thanks-to-pollinator-strategy [accessed 29/4/2021].

Piper, R. (2021) *Dr. Ross Piper*. Online, Dr. Ross Piper. Available from: https://www.rosspiper.net/2020/01/10/saproxylic-beetles/ [accessed 7/10/2021].

Plantlife (2019) *Every Flower Counts – 2019 Results*. Online, Plantlife. Available from: https://www.plantlife.org.uk/everyflowercounts/2019-results/ [accessed 7/4/2021].

Plants for a Future (n.d.) *Juglans regia*. Online, Plants for a Future. Available from: https://pfaf.org/user/Plant.aspx?LatinName=Juglans+regia [accessed 10/7/2021].

Pollan, M. (1991) *Second Nature*. London: Bloomsbury Publishing.

Proctor, M. & Yeo, P. F. (1973) *The Pollination of Flowers*. Glasgow: William Collins Sons and Co. Ltd.

Rainer, T. (2018) Planting renaissance. *Garden Design Journal*, August, pp. 25–28.

RHS (2021a) *Mulches and Mulching*. Online, RHS. Available from: https://www.rhs.org.uk/advice/profile?pid=323 [accessed 12/10/2021].

RHS (2021b) *Native and Non-Native Plants for Plant-Dwelling Invertebrates*. Online, RHS. Available from: https://www.rhs.org.uk/advice/profile?PID=1019 [accessed 18 March 2021].

RHS (2021c) *Prairie Planting: Creation and Maintenance*. Online, RHS. Available from: https://www.rhs.org.uk/advice/profile?PID=1025 [accessed 3/5/2021].

RHS (2021d) *RHS Plants for Pollinators*. Online, RHS. Available from: https://www.rhs.org.uk/science/conservation-biodiversity/wildlife/plants-for-pollinators [accessed 13/9/2021].

RHS (2021e) *Wildlife in Gardens*. Online, RHS. Available from: https://www.rhs.org.uk/advice/profile?PID=551 [accessed 28/9/2021].

Rollings, R. (2019) *Six Year Research Study*. Online, Rosybee. Available from: https://www.rosybee.com/research [accessed 18 March 2021].

Rollings, R. & Goulson, D. (2019) Quantifying the attractiveness of garden flowers for pollinators. *Journal of Insect Conservation*, 23, pp. 803–817.

RSPB (n.d.) *Grow Plants for Caterpillars*. Online, RSPB. Available from: https://www.rspb.org.uk/get-involved/activities/nature-on-your-doorstep/garden-activities/growfoodthatcaterpillarslove/ [accessed 6/4/2021].

Russ, A., Rüger, A. & Klenke, R. (2015) Seize the night: European blackbirds (*Turdus merula*) extend their foraging activity under artificial illumination. *Journal of Ornithology*, 156 (1), pp. 123–131.

Salisbury, A., Armitage, J., Bostock, H., Perry, J., Tatchell, M. & Thompson, K. (2015) Editor's Choice: Enhancing gardens as habitats for flower-visiting aerial insects (pollinators): should we plant native or exotic species? *Journal of Applied Ecology*, 52 (5), pp. 1156–1164.

Salisbury, A., Al-Beidh, S., Armitage, J., Bird, S., Bostock, H., Platoni, A., Tatchell, M., Thompson, K. & Perry, J. (2017) Enhancing gardens as habitats for plant-associated invertebrates: should we plant native or exotic species? *Biodiversity and Conservation*, 26 (11), pp. 2657–2673.

Salisbury, A., Al-Beidh, S., Armitage, J., Bird, S., Bostock, H., Platoni, A., Tatchell, M., Thompson, K. & Perry, J. (2020) Enhancing gardens as habitats for soil-surface-active invertebrates: should we plant native or exotic species? *Biodiversity and Conservation*, 29 (1), pp. 129–151.

Sansone, A. (2020) *11 Plant Combos You Should Grow Side-By-Side*. Online, Country Living. Available from: https://www.countryliving.com/gardening/news/g4188/companion-planting/ [accessed 20/10/2021].

Schofield, K., Pettitt, T. R., Tappin, A. D., Rollinson, G. K. & Fitzsimons, M. F. (2019) Biochar incorporation increased nitrogen and carbon retention in a waste-derived soil. *Science of the Total Environment*, 690 (November), pp. 1228–1236.

Smithson, A. & Smithson, P. (1990) *The 'As Found' and the 'Found'*. Online, The MIT Press. Available from: http://designtheory.fiu.edu/readings/smithson_as_found.pdf [accessed 2/8/2021].

Spencer, T. (2020) *Supernaturalistic: The New Perennial Pond Garden*. Online, The New Perennialist. Available from: https://www.thenewperennialist.com/supernaturalistic-the-new-perennial-pond-garden/ [accessed 10/4/2021].

Springwatch (2021) *How are Our Beloved Blue Tits Faring this Spring?* Online, BBC. Available from: https://www.bbc.co.uk/blogs/natureuk/entries/6c4186c6-fcdd-4285-ae69-4b6e458d35ed [accessed 28/6/2021].

Stone, E. (n.d.) *Bats and Lighting Overview of Current Evidence and Mitigation*. Online, cdn.bats.org.uk. Available from: https://cdn.bats.org.uk/uploads/pdf/Bats_and_Lighting_-_Overview_of_evidence_and_mitigation_-_2014_UPDATE.pdf?v=1541085191 [accessed 18/10/2021].

Swailes, J. (2016) *Field Sketching and the Experience of Landscape*. Abingdon and New York: Routledge.

Takkis, K., Tscheulin, T., Tsalkatis, P. & Petanidou, T. (2015) Climate change reduces nectar secretion in two common Mediterranean plants. *AoB PLANTS*, 7.

The Arboricultural Association (2019) *Help for Tree Owners*. Online, The Arboricultural Association. Available from: https://www.trees.org.uk/Help-Advice/Help-for-Tree-Owners [accessed 8/8/2021].

The Arboricultural Association (2021) *Biosecurity*. Online, The Arboricultural Association. Available from: https://www.trees.org.uk/Help-Advice/Biosecurity-Guidance [accessed 12/10/2021].

The Bat Conservation Trust (2021) *Flight, Food and Echolocation*. Online, The Bat Conservation Trust. Available from: https://www.bats.org.uk/about-bats/flight-food-and-echolocation [accessed 7/10/2021].

Thompson, K. (2007) *No Nettles Required: The Truth About Wildlife Gardening*. London: Transworld Publishers.

Thompson, K. (2008) *An Ear to the Ground: Understanding Your Garden*. London: Transworld Publishers.

Thompson, K. & Head, S. (2020) *Gardens as a Resource for Wildlife*. Online, Wildlife Gardening Forum. Available from: http://www.wlgf.org/The%20garden%20Resource.pdf [accessed 28/9/2021].

Tilley, C. (1994) *A Phenomenology of Landscape: Places, Paths and Monuments*. Oxford: Berg.

Tonhasca, A. (2020) *The Graveyard Shift: The Elusive Side of Pollination*. Online, Scottish Pollinators. Available from: https://scottishpollinators.wordpress.com/2020/10/26/the-graveyard-shift-the-elusive-side-of-pollination/ [accessed 7/10/2021].

Tuinen Mien Ruys (2013) *Marsh Garden*. Online, Tuinen Mien Ruys. Available from: https://www.tuinenmienruys.nl/en/marsh-garden-1990/ [accessed 20/5/2021].

Twining, C. W., Shipley, J. R. & Winkler, D. W. (2018) Aquatic insects rich in omega-3 fatty acids drive breeding success in a widespread bird. *Ecology Letters*, 21 (12), pp. 1812–1820.

United Nations (2019) *Sustainable Development Goals: UN Report: Nature's Dangerous Decline 'Unprecedented'; Species Extinction Rates 'Accelerating'*. Online, United Nations.

Available from: https://www.un.org/sustainabledevelopment/blog/2019/05/nature-decline-unprecedented-report/ [accessed 29/9/2021].

University of Cambridge (2017) *Petals Produce a 'Blue Halo' that Helps Bees Find Flowers*. Online, University of Cambridge Research. Available from: https://www.cam.ac.uk/research/news/petals-produce-a-blue-halo-that-helps-bees-find-flowers [accessed 27/9/2021].

University of Wisconsin (n.d.) *Rain Gardens: A Guide for Homeowners and Landscapers*. Online, University of Wisconsin. Available from: https://www.uwsp.edu/cnr-ap/UWEXLakes/Documents/ecology/shoreland/raingarden/RainGardenManualPrint-small.pdf [accessed 10/6/2021].

Voigt, C., Azam, C., Dekker, J., Ferguson, J., Fritze, M., Gazaryan, S., Hölker, F., Jones, G., Leader, N., Lewanzik, D., Limpens, H., Mathews, F., Rydell, J., Schofield, H., Spoelstra, K. & Zagmajster, M. (2018) *Guidelines for Consideration of Bats in Lighting Projects*. UNEP/EUROBATS 8.

Walling, L. (2000) The myriad plant responses to herbivores. *Journal of Plant Growth Regulation* 19, pp. 195–216.

Warner, A. (n.d.) *All You Ever Wanted to Know About Hedge Laying*. Online, The National Trust. Available from: https://www.nationaltrust.org.uk/buttermere-valley/features/all-you-ever-wanted-to-know-about-hedge-laying [accessed 25/10/2021].

Williams, P., Whitfield, M., Thorne, A., Bryant, S., Fox, G. & Nicolet, P. (2018) *The Pond Book: A Guide to the Management and Creation of Ponds*, 3rd edition. Oxford: The Freshwater Habitats Trust.

Woodland Trust (2013) *Hedges and Hedgerows*. Online, Woodland Trust. Available from: https://www.woodlandtrust.org.uk/media/1808/hedges-and-hedgerows-position-statement.pdf [accessed 25/9/2021].

Woodland Trust (2018) *Nature's Calendar: Tritrophic Phenological Match-Mismatch in Space and Time*. Online, Woodland Trust. Available from: https://naturescalendar.woodlandtrust.org.uk/analysis/research-reports/published-research/tritrophic-phenological-match-mismatch-in-space-and-time/ [accessed 28/6/2021].

Woodland Trust (n.d.-a) *Orchards*. Online, Woodland Trust. Available from: https://www.woodlandtrust.org.uk/trees-woods-and-wildlife/habitats/orchards/ [accessed 11/4/2021].

Woodland Trust (n.d.-b) *Willow, Goat*. Online, Woodland Trust. Available from: https://www.woodlandtrust.org.uk/trees-woods-and-wildlife/british-trees/a-z-of-british-trees/goat-willow/ [accessed 7/10/2021].

Woodland Trust (n.d.-c) *A-Z of British Trees*. Online, Woodland Trust. Available from: https://www.woodlandtrust.org.uk/trees-woods-and-wildlife/british-trees/a-z-of-british-trees/ [accessed 2/6/2021].

WRAP (2021) *Using BSI PAS 100 Compost in Combination with Other Recycled Materials*. Online, WRAP. Available from: http://archive.wrap.org.uk/content/using-bsi-pas-100-compost-combination-other-recycled-materials [accessed 2/7/2021].

WWT (n.d.) *A Guide to Native Pond Plants...What Not to Choose*. Online, WWT Wildfowl and Wetlands Trust. Available from: https://www.wwt.org.uk/discover-wetlands/gardening-for-wetlands/a-guide-to-native-pond-plants [accessed 15/5/2021].

INDEX